CUCUMBERS IN
A FLOWERPOT

D1601282

CUCUMBERS IN A FLOWERPOT

by Alice Skelsey

Illustrated by Judith Sutton

New and Revised Edition

Formerly FARMING IN A FLOWERPOT

Workman Publishing, New York

Library of Congress Cataloging in Publication Data
Skelsey, Alice Fulton, 1926–
Cucumbers in a flowerpot.
Rev. ed. of: Farming in a flowerpot. 1975.
1. Vegetable gardening. 2. Fruit-culture.
3. Container gardening. I. Title.
SB324.4.S53 1984   635   83-40551   ISBN 0-89480-729-3

Cover illustration: Jackie Geyer
Book illustrations: Judith Sutton
Book design: Susan Aronson Stirling

Workman Publishing Company
1 West 39 Street
New York, New York 10018

Manufactured in the United States of America
First printing April 1984
10 9 8 7 6 5 4 3 2 1

To Gloria and Fred Huckaby—
Master Gardeners in and around the house...
as generous with help in learning and
writing about container farming as with the
harvests from their gardens.

Contents

Contents

WHAT'S IN STORE FOR THE CITY FARMER

A packet of seeds, a pot of soil, a spot of sunshine—that's all you need to become a city farmer. Why be content with philodendron and ivy just because you live in an apartment or town house? You should be growing fruits and vegetables instead!

Yes, you *can* farm in flowerpots. You can have your "houseplants" and eat them, too. Horticulturists have developed fruits and vegetables particularly suited to growing in containers—varieties that take only a minimal amount of space and attention.

Clearly, container gardeners are no longer pioneers. Look at all the good things that have happened in the world of container gardening since this book first appeared. Many more dwarf, midget and mini versions of all kinds of vegetables and fruits have been developed and are much more widely available. Vining crops such as squash and melons that normally require lots of space to sprawl have been turned into compact bush plants that are more content to stay in bounds. All kinds of fruit trees and bushes have been condensed in size. Even a blueberry variety— Tophat—has been developed especially for growing in a container.

These smaller, more compact versions of familiar plants do not mean that the fruits or vegetables themselves need be less desirable. Yield, flavor and overall quality are top considerations of crop breeders. The fruit from dwarf trees, for example, is often comparable in size to that from standard-size trees—in some cases, even larger. Many commercial growers, in fact, have themselves switched to dwarf trees. (Some experimental orchards are now planted with peach trees only 18 inches high!)

New containers specifically designed for food crops can also be found. Consider the Vegi-Tub: It weighs only 5 pounds but is 21 inches high and big enough for 300 carrots or 3 tomato plants, with a molded bottom designed to hold 5 support stakes firmly in place.

You'll discover that a tender young spring carrot tastes little like its store-bought cousin. Strawberries eaten minutes after leaving your high-rise "patch" are definitely sweeter, both in flavor and in the satisfaction of knowing you grew them yourself. Potted tomatoes, peppers and lettuce are beautiful to behold and offer a ready supply of salads right from your own balcony or patio. All are possible for apartment dwellers or anyone with limited garden space to grow.

While the economics of farming in flowerpots may be a tossup for most crops (tomatoes, green peppers and cucumbers often more than pay their way, though), who could set a monetary value on the pleasure derived from growing your own. Nothing short of moving to the country could do more to freshen the spirits and surroundings of the cramped city dweller. Whether you're an inveterate "green-thumber" or entirely inexperienced, you'll find growing your own fruits and vegetables at home a rewarding and delicious experience.

All sorts of convenience products now on the market make gardening anything but a chore. You will find prepackaged soil mixes that are far more reliable than ordinary garden soil, plants that can be moved from one environment to another (pot and all) without ever disturbing a root, and carefully formulated fertilizers for "instant" feedings. With all kinds and varieties of plants for the city farmer to try, excitement and suspense are built into each new season. Could you recognize the beautiful gray-green leaves and lavender flowers of the eggplant? Do you really recall the flavor of a fresh-picked tomato? Equipped with a patio, balcony, doorstep or even a window sill, plus sunlight for a good part of the day, your "farm" will know no limits. So tell your African violets, geraniums and philodendrons to move over and make room, and try a few new crops each spring.

SEVEN STEPS TO FARMING IN A FLOWERPOT

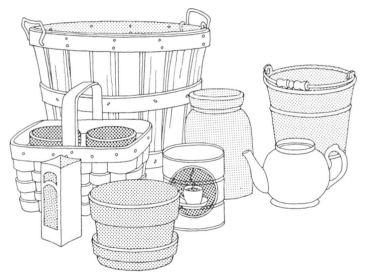

1. Choosing Containers for Your Crops

To get the most out of your "land," it's important to match the container to the crop. Obviously, a container should be large enough to hold the plant and its fruit when it reaches maturity. But sometimes it is difficult to judge just how big a plant will grow, seed packet information notwithstanding. Just one leaf lettuce plant, for example, while starting out as the tiniest of seeds and emerging as the most fragile of seedlings, can grow to overflow a gallon container. A normal-size eggplant will need a container as large as a half-bushel basket (four gallons), not so much for the bushlike plant but to accommodate its fruit, which can be large and heavy.

On the other hand, some plants do not do well in large containers. They actually seem to prefer a pot that is small in relation to their size at maturity. A large tomato plant can thrive in a two-gallon container provided it is well-balanced and won't topple when the plant grows top-heavy. A miniature tomato plant can be grown in an eight- or ten-inch flowerpot.

Since decisions on container size cannot always be based on advance knowledge of the mature plant and its fruit, you must learn from your own observations of the plant's growth habits. The encouraging aspect of such "by-guess-and-by-golly" gardening is that it takes little additional effort or expense to adjust crops and containers from year to year as you gain experience. The novice with no idea of where to start should first consult the recommendations for each fruit and vegetable in the individual sections devoted to them. The following table will also be of help in visualizing the approximate capacity of different types of containers.

Ordinary red clay pots are the preference of many gardeners. These range in size from 2 to 14 inches

	quart	half-gallon	gallon	10-gallon	20-gallon	30-gallon
Milk carton	✓	✓	✓			
One-pound coffee can	✓					
Two-pound coffee can		✓				
Plastic ice cream carton	✓	✓				
Plastic bleach container	✓	✓	✓			
Garbage can				✓	✓	✓

(diameter measured across the inside top) and have corresponding saucers for catching drainage water. They are widely available, decorative, relatively inexpensive and ideal for most plants. Clay pots are heavy, however, and this could be a problem if intended for roofs or other locations where weight must be considered, or if pots must be moved often.

Plastic pots can be found in comparable sizes and prices. Choose them in dark green to go best with food crops. Tin cans will also work if holes are punched in the sides of the can near the bottom, to allow for drainage. But they would probably be most satisfactory as a liner or container within a container.

For trees, select a container large enough to last a number of years so you won't have to go looking for a new one every season. Some trees, such as orange, lemon and lime, do well in small containers. A gallon-size pot will last at least three or four years. Other fruit trees, such as dwarf peaches, have a large root system—as large or larger than the aboveground part of the tree when it's purchased. Such a tree must obviously start out in a tub roomy enough to accommodate its roots.

Here's a table of sizes and approximate prices. The latter will vary somewhat in different localities; garden centers in discount stores usually offer the lowest prices but not always the widest selection of sizes.

Large wooden tubs are beautiful but expensive.

SIZE, CAPACITY, AND PRICE OF CLAY POTS			
Diameter Inside Top	Approximate Soil Content	Price Pot	Saucer
2 inches	⅓ cup	$ .25	$ .25
2½ inches	⅔ cup	.29	.29
3 inches	1 cup	.29	.39
4 inches	2½ cups	.39	.49
5 inches	4½ cups	.59	.49
6 inches	2½ quarts	.59	.99
7 inches	3 quarts	.79	1.49
8 inches	1 gallon	1.59	1.99
9 inches	1½ gallons	1.99	1.99
10 inches	2¼ gallons	2.29	2.29
12 inches	3½ gallons	3.99	2.29
14 inches	6 gallons	6.99	2.29

For redwood, figure anywhere from $1.50 to $2 per inch of the tub's diameter—$15 for a 10-inch diameter tub, $45 for a 24-inch. Teakwood or cypress are other possibilities. All of these woods are rot-resistant; soil can be placed into them directly. If a wooden crate or a barrel or box made of pine or oak is selected, the inside should be coated with either creosote, an asphalt paint, or a commercial preparation called Cuprinol to prevent rot. Because wooden containers over 12 inches in diameter can become quite heavy (an 18-inch diameter tub filled with soil could weigh more than 200 pounds), a roller platform should be placed beneath them. These platforms—simply an inch-thick board with ball-bearing casters attached—can be purchased or easily made for $10 to $20.

Barrels can be used for berries. Reproductions of old packing barrels are now widely available. A barrel is a bit of a project to prepare (see Strawberries, page 102) and is heavy when filled, but it makes a wonderful "patch" that will last for years.

Growers with some yard space or convenient access to a roof might consider building a raised bed for a vegetable garden that can really be cultivated and coddled. Caution: Check with the building owner or superintendent before rushing out for supplies—the weight of wet soil and containers can be substantial. A 3-foot-wide, 6-foot-long bed filled with soil 10 inches deep could weigh more than 1,000 pounds. Raised beds can be constructed from 2- × 12-inch redwood boards reinforced at the corners, as illustrated. Although the length of the bed will, of course, depend on the available space, its width should be at least three feet, sufficient to accommodate two or three rows of radishes, lettuce, beets, carrots or onions—a sort of mini truck farm.

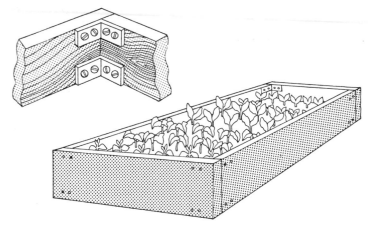

Raised beds can also be made from the large planter boxes available at garden supply houses. If these are used on a balcony, try putting ball-bearing casters on them so they can be moved about to take advantage of the sun. A concrete balcony or asphalt-covered roof reflects a great deal of heat in midsummer. It would be wise to place some sort of dark, light-absorbing plastic or other weatherproof material beneath the planter. Indoor-outdoor carpeting is a good heat absorber, and remnants are easy to find in rug or department stores.

If the container on hand is not as decorative as you might like, then look for a container for the container.

A coffee can inside a wicker basket works fine (line tho bottom of the basket with sphagnum moss, which is available at garden supply shops and most variety stores). Nail kegs (about 14 inches in diameter, 20 inches high) are frequently available at garden shops, hardware stores and lumberyards. Bushel baskets have also made a comeback and are easier to find in both city and suburb than they were a few years ago. They offer yet another planting possibility.

Any kind of plastic bag—freezer, bread, grocery produce, garbage can liner—can make an inexpensive and highly successful container. Plants can remain in the bags from seeding to harvest time. Fill them with a soil mix (see page 29), leaving enough room so that the top of the bag can be fastened with a "twist-um" or folded flat and stapled shut. Place each bag on its side, flatten out the soil, punch holes where the seeds are to go and in the bottom for drainage. Then place the plastic "soil pillows" in some other container to collect runoff when the plants are watered. Your choice of an outer container is nearly limitless since the pillow can be molded to fit any shape or size planter.

Would-be gardeners with absolutely no outdoor space needn't despair. You do have windows. An entire window area can be expanded into a bay-type greenhouse if you own your apartment or town house, say, or if you have a cooperative landlord. These window greenhouse units can be purchased commercially, custom-prefabricated to fit the space or installed from the inside.

An average window can accommodate a greenhouse that will provide 15 to 20 square feet of growing area. (Local ordinance might prohibit such overhang; tenants should check this out before placing any orders.) There are also tiny window sill greenhouses that can provide just-right growing conditions for germinating seeds or pampering delicate young plants. And, of course, there is always the window sill itself—usually large enough for a pot or two. If not, window sill extenders are available through catalogs, or you can simply widen the sill yourself with the addition of shelving supported by brackets.

To supplement the sills still further, add hanging baskets, indoors or out. What could be nicer for Tiny Tim cherry tomatoes. Wire baskets are quite satisfactory—French wire baskets that salad greens are washed in are practical and decorative. Bicycle baskets (sans bicycle) can also be planted. Line wire baskets with unmilled sphagnum moss which has been thoroughly soaked in water. Pack the wet moss in the basket, lining the bottom and sides with at least an inch-and-a-half thickness of moss. Then add potting soil and the plant. Cover the topsoil with another layer of moss, which will help the basket retain moisture longer.

Other kinds of pots can also be hung. Holes can be drilled for chains in wooden ones; ceramic pots can be suspended in a rope cradle. If you are into macramé both simple and elaborate hangings can be designed, and in colors to suit yourself.

The containers and their crops will do much to brighten the décor of a balcony, patio or doorstep, as well as the rooms of your home. You can go op, mod, traditional—whatever your fancy. But do, always, let the plants take center stage. You will find that plain clay pots, pails and stone jars are far more practical (and easier to live with) than the philodendron-in-a-coffee-grinder type of planter.

Take a tour of the dime or hardware store. The housewares department is a good place to find inexpensive containers, often of excellent design. Look for bowls, tubs and baskets; for kettles, pots and pans; for boxes and buckets. How about a colander for something a bit offbeat but not too "cute"? Lined with plastic (a few holes repunched in the bottom) and filled with a layer of gravel, the soil and a planting of parsley, it will be charming and practical—unpretentious and perfectly suited for its use.

Clay, wood, pottery, plastic, metal, Styrofoam—almost anything can be used for plants, provided it has adequate holes for drainage. Drainage capacity and porosity of container material are the major distinctions among different types of containers. These two factors mainly determine the amount and frequency of watering needed. For plants to obtain both air and water—which they must have to survive—the roots must be alternately dry and wet. Extremes of either, of course, affect the health of the plants adversely.

Make sure the container you choose has adequate drainage. If it is less than 10 inches in diameter, one ½-

inch diameter hole is enough. Containers over 10 inches in diameter—other than clay pots, which are quite porous—should have three or four ½-inch holes. If the container is porous, air and water can enter through it and less provision for runoff is required. The following paragraphs summarize the qualities of porosity and drainage in various types of containers.

⧉ **Ordinary Clay Pot.** Clay is porous, allowing air and water to pass through the sides of the pot to the soil inside; existing drainage holes are adequate in size and number.

⧉ **Wooden Container.** Less porous than clay; often comes without a drainage hole in the bottom, in which case holes may be drilled; otherwise, a two-inch layer of coarse gravel or perlite should be placed in the bottom before adding soil.

⧉ **Plastic Container.** Not at all porous. Less frequent watering is needed, which can be an advantage if you are often away for weekends.

⧉ **Styrofoam Pots.** Air porous but not water porous; less frequent watering is required than with clay pots.

⧉ **Plastic Bags.** Neither air nor water porous; since there is practically no evaporation from a sealed plastic container, less frequent watering is required.

Raised Bed. Because of its large surface area, porosity of the container material is less of a factor than with pots and smaller containers. For good drainage and air circulation, place a two-inch layer of coarse gravel in the bottom before adding soil; or use a two-inch layer of a light porous stone called featherock (available at lumberyards) if weight is a critical factor, as it is likely to be on roofs. Styrofoam packing materials or even old Styrofoam coolers crumbled to peanut-size pieces can also be used for drainage. There is a high rate of evaporation in raised beds and daily watering is essential.

Hanging Baskets. A basket dries out very quickly and will likely require daily watering. It should be hung where it can be easily retrieved for watering, which is best done by submerging the basket up to the soil level in a container of water and letting it soak for a few minutes. Allow it to drain before rehanging indoors or over a walkway if no provision has been made to catch drainage.

Hanging Pots. Usually there is an attached saucer to catch drainage water, but even so, hanging pots dry out rather quickly and require daily watering. In planting hanging baskets and pots, leave half an inch or so between the top of the soil and the rim of the container. Otherwise, water will spill over the side of the container before it soaks through.

As your farm expands, and it will, you may find that grouping the containers on a tea cart, a kitchen utility cart, a child's wagon, a wheelbarrow or a heavy piece of plywood (¾-inch, exterior grade) with ball-bearing casters attached will make the job of caring for your crops easier. On chilly nights in early spring and fall, or when there is inclement weather, you'll be able to move the plants to a more protected place—to a sheltered corner or indoors, if need be. Come bad weather, you'll be thankful that you can roll your garden to safety and not have to depend on a hastily rigged plastic shield that may quickly be blown to shreds.

One further word on gardening space. Many apartment buildings have outside fire escapes, which may appear to be just the spot for a pot or planter. However, the ordinances of most cities prohibit placement of containers of any kind on fire escapes. Some local authorities allow baskets or planters to be hung from a fire escape if they do not interfere with egress from the building. Check your local fire prevention authority.

2. Improving on the Good Earth

To get started, you really don't need much more than a pot, some dirt and a seed to put in it. But though getting the container is relatively simple, putting your hands on some dirt can be something of a problem Sometimes, the only real dirt an urbanite encounters (other than the airborne variety) is that owned by the city in its public parks—and officials frown on citizens carrying it home in flowerpots. So if you must be a real dirt gardener, persuade a suburban or farmer friend to part with some topsoil, rather than resorting to furtive trips at dusk with your son's pail and shovel.

Real dirt is fine for plants safely past the sprouting and seedling stage and ready for transplant. Or for use with rootstock of dwarf citrus and other fruit trees. (To lighten its weight and texture, mix in some artificial soil.) But beware. Even the best of garden soils should be sterilized before being used for seeds.

Probably the greatest danger in the use of unsterilized soil is the likelihood of a fungus disease carried in the soil. Called "damping-off," this affliction is a depressing and discouraging experience. The seeds sprout, vigorous plants emerge and then, quite suddenly, the stems shrink and shrivel just above the soil level. Those little plants that once held such bright promise collapse and die almost overnight.

To avoid "damping-off" and other equally disastrous though perhaps less dramatic "happenings," you must sterilize the honest-to-goodness kind of dirt before you use it as potting soil for seeds. The usual home method is to bake it in the oven in a flat pan, for at least one hour, at 215°F. But before you decide to test your culinary skill, let us say that it is not as simple a job as all that. It can, in fact, make an awful mess—

and a worse smell. Moreover, you should wait at least two weeks before using the soil. This allows the ammonia released in the heating process to escape.

For these reasons, and considering the limited amount of gardening they do, most container gardeners find it expedient to buy either a commercially-prepared growing medium (variously referred to as artificial, synthetic or formula potting soils) or the readily available ingredients that they can mix themselves.

The packaged artificial soils have many advantages: they are specially formulated to provide a good growing medium for your plants; they are free from disease organisms, nematodes (a root-attacking pest) and weed seed; and they are much lighter than ordinary soil, making it much easier to move the container about, if need be. Though an 8-inch plastic pot containing regular soil might weigh about 10 pounds, the same pot filled with artificial soil would weigh only about 4½ pounds. The texture is also light and porous, allowing root crops to develop well and water to drain properly.

Artificial soils are available in various quantities, priced from under $1 for a quart to about $25 for a 2½-bushel bag. A bushel will provide enough soil for eight 1-gallon containers. Some soil mixes include nutrients to nourish the plants for several weeks; others need to have nutrients added as soon as the seeds sprout. Potting mix designed for African violets is not suitable for vegetables, as its texture is too fine.

For those who wish to mix their own soil, the following "recipe" will make 7 or 8 bushels—enough to launch an ambitious gardening venture or to divide with neighbors and friends. The ingredients are available in garden stores in the approximate sizes listed (with the exception of limestone) and in smaller sizes as well, for those whose requirements are less.

Soil Mix

One 4-cubic-foot bag of sphagnum moss

One 4-cubic-foot bag of vermiculite

Two and one-half pounds of limestone (about the smallest prepackaged bag you can buy is 10 pounds, but limestone is inexpensive— under a dollar a bag)

and either

Two pounds of a tomato food type fertilizer, a 6-18-6 or 5-10-10 formula, for example (see A Balanced Diet, page 44, to unravel the mystery of these numbers, which aren't really as confusing as they seem)

or

Two pounds of 5-10-5 fertilizer plus one pound of superphosphate (0-20-0)

Pour these ingredients together in a pile on a piece of canvas or heavy plastic (press the shower curtain into service if nothing else is available). The balcony, porch, or as a last resort, the kitchen or bathroom is your work area. Use hot water to moisten the ingredients as you add each one to the pile. The water cuts down on the dust, and if it is hot the moss absorbs it better.

Don't try to stir the mixture to blend it—it's too much of a job. Instead, lift it by shovelfuls. Use a sturdy dustpan if you don't have the right tool on hand (and it's hard to imagine you will if you live in an apartment). You'll find the mixing a bit hard on the back, but carry on through the pile, picking up a little of each ingredient and then putting it down in another spot to form a new pile. Repeat the whole process to put the pile back where it was before. If you are stirring up more dust than your nose can stand, sprinkle on a little more water. Move the pile one more time, and you should have it well mixed. And now that you know the procedure for mixing your own, you may well decide to buy the stuff already packaged.

3. Selecting and Sowing Seed

Individual packages of vegetable seed are displayed on racks not only in garden and nursery centers, but also in grocery, variety and hardware stores. The selections usually include several varieties of the most commonly grown vegetables. If your seed-buying will be limited to an item or two—a packet of radishes and one of lettuce, for example—It makes sense to buy from the rack. (When you do, check to see that the date stamped on the packet is the current planting year. The date is your guarantee that the seed you buy is fresh and viable.)

For more ambitious gardening than the seed rack offers (and why not?) do your shopping through the seed catalogs, too. Write to one or two seed houses (names and addresses of a number of seed companies are listed on pages 133 to 138). Catalogs are usually prepared for distribution around December or January, so you can shop at your leisure, make selections, order and have the plant material delivered to you in plenty of time for spring or prespring planting.

Within the last few years, many fruit and vegetable varieties have been developed especially for container gardening, or for the gardener with a pocket-size piece of land. There are now dwarf and miniature fruits and vegetables of almost every kind—peach, cucumber, melon, even corn. Without a catalog to browse through, you'll miss out on the wide selection of potential crops and the new and improved varieties for container gardening that come along each year. The catalogs are also fascinating to read and the true farmer—whether he measures his land by the acre or the inch—always saves a few winter evenings for these informative and colorful publications.

Seeds for some crops can be sown directly into the containers in which they will mature, but other crops are started in small individual pots or in "flats" (fairly large shallow boxes 2 or 3 inches deep). After these plants reach seedling stage, they are "potted up" (transferred to a larger container). Consult the instructions pertaining to individual crops at the end of this book and also the seed packet instructions to determine whether to plant directly into permanent containers or to sow first in smaller pots.

If the crop dictates planting small first, your initial sowing can be in most any container on hand, although a flat accommodates more seeds and is easier to handle than a deep pot. An oblong cake pan would be fine. If it's your best or one-and-only, line it with plastic to prevent discoloration. The deeper foil pans that frozen foods come in make good flats, too.

Some provlsion must be made for drainage, however. Although it is desirable to have drainage holes in the bottom, it is not absolutely necessary. A ½-inch layer of perlite or small-size gravel in the bottom will effect satisfactory drainage. Add a level layer of potting soil 1½ to 2 inches deep, moisten the soil and let it settle a bit. Now sow the seeds on the surface, spacing them according to seed packet instructions. Cover the seeds with the appropriate amount of damp potting soil. Firm the soil in place, tamping it lightly with the bottom of a water glass or with your hand.

Since once in a great while a seed fails to germinate, sow about twice the number of seeds as the number of plants desired. You will, no doubt, have many more seeds than you need in each packet. Don't go overboard and plant them all. Any leftovers can be kept for another year. Just store them in a cool airy place; as long as they have air but no moisture, they will continue to live, but be dormant. (Put the packets in a small jar, punch a couple of holes in the lid and store them on a bottom shelf in the refrigerator, away from the ice compartment.)

After the seeds are planted, cover the entire flat with clear plastic film but don't let it touch the seedbed. The film will help provide a properly humid atmosphere for seed growth. You will not need to add additional water until the seeds have sprouted. As a matter of fact, check every few days to make certain that the soil is not too moist or mildew will begin to grow. If it appears, remove the film and put the flat in

SEVEN STEPS TO FARMING IN A FLOWERPOT

full sun for a few hours so that the soil will dry out promptly. Best practice, of course, is not to use too much water to begin with—only enough to moisten the soil. Place the flat in a warm place (65° to 75°) not in direct sunlight or near direct heat.

Now begins the breathless period of waiting for the first bit of green. The time required for germination (beginning of growth) varies with individual plants; the seed packet almost always provides this information. Most seeds seem to germinate more quickly in the dark, though a few prefer the light. If the seed packet does not state the plant's preference, gamble on the dark. Placing a newspaper over the top of the plastic-covered flat for the germination period specified on the seed packet is a good idea—although you'll probably find yourself peeking several times a day "to see if they've come up yet." When they do, the first thing to appear will be a tender white loop, sometimes fat, sometimes thin, as the stem of the plant begins to lift itself from the soil.

Remove the newspaper and the plastic film and give the flat full light but NO direct sun. In another day the stems will be up nicely, possibly half an inch tall. By now you may need to add water to keep the soil slightly moist; do so lightly with a sprinkler-type watering can or a clothes sprinkler. (Water poured on directly in a heavy stream displaces the lightweight soil and can disturb the plants' growth.)

In another day or so the first leaves will unfold. These are called the "heart leaves"; they are followed

34

in three or four days by two more leaves. These are called "true leaves," distinguished from the heart leaves in that their shape and texture is representative of the mature plant foliage. At this stage the plants are called seedlings.

Because you sowed more seeds than the number of plants you really want or have room for, you now must thin out the surplus seedlings. This should be done when the seedlings are large enough for their leaves to touch their neighbors (except for lettuce and several other salad greens). However heartless this task seems, it's basic to good farming. If you are to provide your seedlings with the best opportunity for growth, you must ruthlessly eliminate any excess competition for food, water and growing room.

The best tool for thinning seedlings is a pair of thin, sharp scissors (manicure, seamstress or barber shears work fine). Reach between the plants and snip

—true leaf
—heart leaf

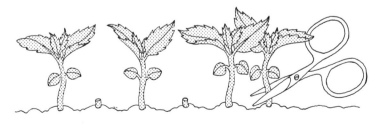

off each unnecessary seedling at the soil line. Do not thin by pulling the seedlings out by their heads, for no matter how tiny they are, their removal can disturb the root systems of the plants that are to remain.

And don't try to save extra seedlings for transplant. In the first place, you already have all the plants you can handle, but more important, transplanted or weeded-out seedlings have a high percentage of failures. It is usually far better just to dispose of the surplus.

When the seedlings have four or six true leaves (two or three pairs) or begin to crowd each other, it is time to transplant them into a larger container. Your objective is to accomplish the transplanting with as little shock to the roots of the plant as possible. So have the individual containers in which you want the young plants to continue growth all ready before you touch a leaf.

The containers should, of course, be clean. Place a piece of mesh screen or a shard (a piece of broken clay pot, the curved side facing down so that the water drains under and out) in the bottom of the container to cover the drainage holes; this will allow the water to run out, but will keep the next layer of gravel from plugging up the hole or the soil from coming out. Next, add about ½ to 1 inch of perlite, gravel or pebbles. Actually, anything that is nondecayable and nonpacking will do—marbles, bottle caps, broken bits of pottery or those white plastic peanuts used widely as packing material. Finally, add the soil mix, up to about two-thirds full. This is the stage at which you can use regular garden dirt.

Have the flat slightly damp, so that when the young plants are separated and lifted out, at least some soil will cling to their roots. Use an old kitchen fork to break the soil about an inch or so away from and all around the young plant. Then with a lifting, wedging action, gently lift the plant up and out of the soil and, handling it by the leaves (so as not to bruise the tender stem), place it immediately into the prepared container. If the flat is a frozen-food pan, it can be cut apart with an old pair of scissors and the plants lifted out with a spatula. Don't worry too much about setting the plant at the proper depth. With the exception of strawberries and trees, this is not a critical factor for most plants. Most vegetable crops should be set a little deeper in the permanent location than they were in the seedbed, and tomatoes profit by being set with half of the stem below the soil line.

Now add more potting soil up to an inch or so of the top of the container. Firm the soil with your hands—firming down into the pot rather than around the stem of the plant. Then set the container into a larger one to soak up water, or water with a sprinkler-type can from above. Either way, as moisture enters, the soil will settle, possibly half an inch. Add enough additional soil to bring the level back to within an inch or so of the top.

A much more convenient route from seed to seedling stage, and one that avoids all the bother of transplanting, is through the use of individual seedling pots. Small 1-inch cubes made up of compressed soil mix and plant food are available. Simply moisten the cube and press the seed into the top of it. The seedling is nourished from a steady supply of food provided by the cube as it disintegrates. Seedling and cube can be easily transplanted.

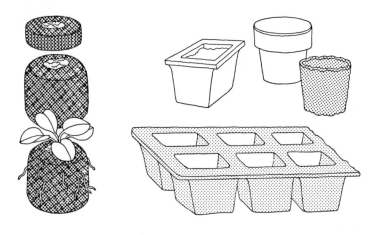

Small peat pots made of compressed peat moss and wood fiber are also widely available. Fill the peat pot with soil mix and plant the seeds. When the seedlings reach transplant stage, soak the peat pot and cut away the bottom. Then put the seedling, with its peat pot band around it, into the soil in your larger or permanent container. The plant roots will have ready access to the new soil from the bottom, while the peat pot band will gradually disintegrate, nurturing the plant in the process. Peat pots are available at garden supply houses and in many variety stores at 5¢ to 10¢

each, depending on the number, size and kind you buy. They range in size from 1½ to 4 inches in diameter. Another type of peat pot comes as a compressed disc, which, when soaked in water, expands into a small, 1-inch pot complete with planting medium (soil mix) and nutrients; all you add is the seed.

Cardboard egg containers are also good for sowing seed. Each half provides a separate "pot" for 12 plants. The carton may be cut apart and each "pot" transplanted to its permanent container. The pressed cardboard bottom of the carton should be cut away as with the peat pot.

Still another way to start seeds is to use preplanted containers. Usually plastic, these containers hold the growing medium and initial nutrients. The seeds either accompany the kit or are already in place. In the latter case, you merely take the container home, punch holes in the clear plastic lid, water and wait. A number of vegetables are available in this type of planter at grocery, drug, dime, novelty and hardware stores. The choice of varieties is limited, however.

A separate pot for each seedling, especially one that decomposes after it is planted, repays the extra investment many times over, not only in the successful handling of plants, but also in time and convenience. But whether you go the "flat" or the "peat pot" route, the important thing is that the plant's growth not be interrupted. Once you get the plant started, growth should proceed steadily. Time lost in transplanting plus the shock to the plant's system will take their toll.

One further caution: After one or two unseasonably mild days in February or March, all gardeners are hard to restrain. The city farmer is no exception and must be especially patient. If seeds are sown too early, the plants will reach transplant stage and be ready for the great outdoors well before the weatherman allows. Plants at this stage will not continue to thrive as they should if they have to remain indoors. Therefore, do not sow the seeds any sooner than six to eight weeks before they can be safely moved outdoors. Call your local National Weather Service station (listed in the phone book under the U.S. Government, Department of Commerce) and ask them for the last predicted frost date in your area. After this date, plants can be safely moved outdoors. Put the seedlings out for an hour or two the first day (in a shaded area) and gradually increase the period of exposure, so that by the end of a week they have grown accustomed to the temperature change and the more direct rays of the sun. This process of acclimation is called "hardening." If the sunlight is very intense, you should rig up a device to shade the seedlings. Suggestions for sunshades are discussed in the next chapter.

4. Shedding Light
on the Subject

Once you begin to farm—whether on your balcony, patio, window sill or roof—you will become acutely sensitive to changes in the sun's position in the sky as the summer progresses. What was a bright spot on the balcony in May, may not be so in August, or vice versa. Before deciding definitely on what crops to grow, consider rather carefully the amount of sunlight available for the plants. If your "farm" faces east, there will

be morning sunlight, but the spot will be shaded from the afternoon sun by your building. If you are on the north side, you will probably receive only morning sun, depending somewhat on the time of year. A southern exposure will receive both early morning and late afternoon sun. On the west, of course, you will have no morning sunlight, but will enjoy the long afternoon and twilight rays. Probably the only city garden to receive full sun throughout the day would be a roof or penthouse terrace.

Many crops need full sun, but there are a number of others that can get along with part sun, part shade. To provide their plants with the best possible environment, city farmers can move them about, following the sun's rays as the seasons dictate. The more portable the containers, the greater the flexibility.

Light is a form of energy and some crops need more of it than others. Heading the list are plants that produce fruit—not only peaches or figs, but also egg-plants and green peppers. Root crops, such as radishes and carrots, can get along with less light. Leaf crops, such as lettuce and chard, are the least demanding.

If the amount of sunlight available to the garden is severely limited, you might consider using supplemental light. Scientists have developed fluorescent lamps for indoor use that provide energy in the form that plants can absorb—light rays in the red and blue parts of the spectrum. These fluorescent lamps give off a soft, cool light. Regular incandescent lamps can and do produce energy, but most of it (about 80 percent) is in the form of heat rather than light; the light they emit—in the yellow and green part of the spectrum—is usually not required by vegetable plants until the blossoming stage.

High-intensity fluorescent lamps are of distinct benefit in starting seedlings, which can use as much as 18 hours of light per day. (It is easy to determine when seedlings are not receiving enough light—the plants will grow tall and spindly, stretching their stems toward the light source.)

High-output grow lamps are available through some seed catalogs and at garden and hardware stores. (Brands to choose from include Gro-Lux, Bright Stik and Gro & Sho.) If you have an ordinary fluorescent lamp, it can also be used.

Lamps range from simple, fluorescent tubes at $2,

which you can use in your own fixture, to multiple-tube, multi-plant tray stands that cost as much as $250. Some fixtures combine fluorescent and incandescent lights. Read the descriptions carefully to decide which will best suit your needs. Industrial-type fixtures that come with attached reflectors and are wired for standard current can be found in almost any hardware store for $10 to $15.

It is probably wise to think small at the beginning. Experiment first with growing seedlings under a single small unit. The results will probably be so pleasing—sturdy, compact plants—that you will want to go on to more elaborate fixtures as your living space allows. Keep in mind that houseplants can also be grown along with your crops (and should be, for the fetching combinations and color they can add to a plant grouping), and many do splendidly under lights. Gardening under lights is, in fact, a hobby in itself.

Remember, however, that even the best supplemental light has its limits. For example, grow lamps would not be practical as the main source of light for bringing tomatoes into fruit—they simply do not come anywhere near to delivering the equivalent energy of the sun. On the other hand, artificial light can be used successfully to establish the sturdiest, healthiest seedlings you have ever seen, to produce leaf crops, to keep an herb garden thriving or to give a boost to or lengthen the daylight time of other crops.

The container gardener who has full sunlight available may have his problems, too. Full sunlight can be a mixed blessing for crops on a patio, balcony or other spot where the reflection from brick, concrete and paving can produce intense heat. Cool-season crops—lettuce or radishes, for example—are not heat-hardy and will not survive such a situation. An eggplant or tomato is more heat-tolerant, but must still be protected from intense heat.

Various precautions can be taken to protect plants during the hottest part of the midsummer days. One way to conquer the sun is to cut out a number of one-inch strips from an inexpensive beach umbrella, thus creating a slatted sunshade over the plants. Heat-absorbing materials placed under and in back of plants can also help cut down on reflected heat. For roof gardens, protection can be inexpensively contrived with bamboo shades, awnings or a sheet of opaque fiberglass.

For the cool-season plants, simply start them early enough to beat the heat. Have them safely raised and eaten before the dog days of summer arrive. (The Growth Chart on pages 131 and 132 indicates the preferred growing season for various vegetables.)

5. Serving a Balanced Diet

Plants need a balanced diet just as people do, and you will find that they are heavy feeders. However, though they like to be fed before they get too hungry, they do not like to be stuffed. A steady supply of essential nutrients is what is needed to keep them thriving.

The three main elements in a plant's diet are nitrogen, phosphorus and potassium. The numbers which identify fertilizer formulas—whether 20-10-4, 4-10-6, 5-10-5 or any of the many other combinations—refer to the percentage of these three elements in the formula. The numbers are always given in this order: the percentage of nitrogen first, phosphorus second and potassium third.

Different plants require different amounts of these elements, and the same plant's needs also vary depending upon the stage of its development. Nitrogen, for example, is believed to be most important when a plant is growing fast and producing foliage. When the plant is flowering and setting fruit, it needs phosphorus. Potassium is necessary for healthy roots.

In the most general terms, leafy vegetables—lettuce, spinach, chard—prefer nitrogen for making tender, juicy leaves. Fruit-bearing crops—tomatoes, eggplant, green peppers—respond to phosphorus. Root crops—radishes, carrots, beets—like potassium.

Various trace elements are also important in a plant's diet and the one most often lacking is iron. You may note from time to time that the leaves on your plants are yellowing while the veins remain green. The condition is likely to be chlorosis and can be corrected by the addition of chelated iron to the plant's diet.

Don't let all the hocus-pocus that seems to surround the fertilizer "mystique" unduly alarm you. It does not require deep scientific study. You can, in fact, simply buy plant foods that are formulated specifically for the types of plants you wish to grow. Tomato food, for example, is packaged and labeled as such. It is high in phosphorus and is effective for a number of other crops, as the label will point out. As a matter of fact, if you are to choose just one fertilizer to use, pick one with a proportionately high middle number (for phosphorus) in relation to the other two.

You will find fertilizer packaged in sizes as small as eight ounces. Some fertilizers are to be dissolved in water (one teaspoon or one tablespoon to a gallon of water, for example) and then applied to the plant. Such soluble foods are quickly available to the plant. Other fertilizers come in tablet or pellet form to be pressed into the soil not too close to the plant. These release their nutrients more slowly and over a longer period of time.

When you transplant seedlings, give them a fertilizer treatment and regular feedings thereafter. There are no specific rules for the amount to use or the frequency of application, but a good general guide is to resist the reasoning, "If a little is good, a lot is better." It's just not so. Nitrogen, for example, produces results you can see—and fast! Foliage greens up and grows quickly. The temptation is great to give the plant more than it actually needs or is good for it. Too much nitrogen encourages foliage growth at the expense of flowers and fruit. Unusually dark green, brittle foliage and weak stems are fairly accurate indications of nitrogen overfeeding. Best follow package directions to the letter. These instructions have been worked out carefully to ensure the best performance from the products.

If you have a blender, you can use it to whip up an occasional extra taste treat for your container plants. Put in vegetable peelings, lettuce leaves, eggshells and whatever other attractive garbage you may have on hand. Add water (enough to wind up with a very thin liquid) and then give the whole business a good whirl in the blender. (Most of these mixtures will look awful.)

You can add this health-food treatment to your plants once every few weeks in place of plain watering. The minerals are good for your plants, and recycling at least some organic materials into the garden might ease any vaguely sinful feelings you may have about being dependent upon chemical fertilizers.

If you have even a small piece of Mother Earth to garden in—a window box, even—then kitchen garbage belongs in your garden on a routine basis. Start as soon as space becomes available after harvest in the fall. Chop the kitchen scraps up fine, dig a hole in the garden, dump the chopped mixture in, add a bit of fertilizer, cover back up with dirt and water well. Pick a new spot each time and by frost you'll have a good underlayer of organic matter which, come spring, you can turn up and mix through the soil.

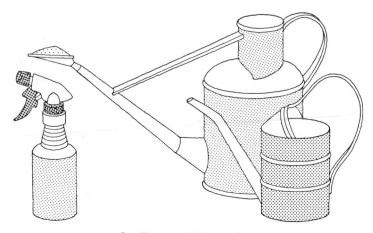

6. Providing for Adequate Water

The novice soon learns—mostly by experience, not reading books—how much water to give his plants. Use your eyes (Does the soil *look* dry? Do the leaves *look* limp?) and also your touch (Does the soil *feel* dry? Do the leaves *feel* parched?). Crops grown in containers dry out quickly from sun and wind, and the smaller the planter, the faster the soil will lose water. Check the containers each day. The soil should not be constantly soggy, but neither should it dry out completely. It should feel slightly moist to the touch. With only a little experience, you'll get the "feel" of it.

You can also learn to judge water content by the weight of the container (if it is small enough to lift comfortably). A container will seem relatively light when the plant needs water. If the container is too large to lift, give it a sharp tap with your knuckles. If there is a hollow, ringing sound, the plant needs water; if there is a dull thump, wait a while.

If plants are outdoors, they will almost surely need daily watering. Give enough water so that it reaches the bottom of the pot and drains through. See that the pots have adequate drainage (drainage hole and layer of perlite, gravel or pebbles) so excess water won't settle around the roots. Keep a saucer (clay, pottery, soup or cereal bowl or pie tin) under the smaller containers. After about 10 to 15 minutes, the container can be lifted and the saucer emptied. This will keep the plant from having "wet feet."

For larger containers, or a group of smaller containers, place the pots on a shallow tray that has been filled with pebbles. A shallow roasting pan works fine. Excess water drains off into the pebbles while the container remains above water level. Indoors, this practice also adds extra moisture to the air, a boon to plants relegated to the dry air of most apartments.

In the city, there's also the problem of soot and other airborne dirt accumulating on your plants (and clogging their pores) unless they are kept wiped clean. Lightly dusting the leaves with a dry cloth rather than a damp one may work better, because some of this gunk is greasy and has a tendency to smear when wet. Pouring water over the plant doesn't work too well, because it takes a good bit of water (as well as care in where and how you splash it) and the method is generally inefficient and messy.

If the stuff that settles on your plants is oily and sticks to the leaves, then use a warm, slightly soapy cloth to give the plant leaves an occasional bath. Follow up by rinsing with a damp cloth, or by putting them in the shower if you can adjust the shower head for a fine mist. If the kitchen or bathroom faucets are close enough, you can rig up an efficient watering and bathing system for your crops by, using a separate shower head attached to rubber tubing fitted onto the regular faucet. Trail the tubing through a window, if you have to, to reach the porch or balcony. Such a portable watering system will save many a step.

If your plants are dropping leaves or if the foliage is turning yellow, the atmosphere may be too dry and they will benefit greatly from misting. Little hand misters are sold in garden or discount stores. If you still have baby's vaporizer on hand, this is an excellent way to increase the humidity of your indoor garden. Use it with just plain water, of course.

7. Tender Loving Care

Surely no one who sows a seed needs to be told that TLC is a built-in part of successful gardening, but for city farmers such commitment is crucial. There's no need to tiptoe in at 2:00 A.M. to see if your seedlings are still breathing, nor must you panic at first sight of a faintly yellow leaf and rush to administer five or six different lifesaving remedies at once. Tender loving care means dependability: that you check on your plants every day; that you water and feed them when necessary; that you provide for their care when you must be away (even one day on a hot roof in midsummer without water could be catastrophic). You must also shelter your plants from wind and storms and searing sun, and wipe their leaves or give them baths when needed.

Keep in mind the limits of your land, and don't overpopulate the plot. City farmers are often guilty of overenthusiasm. One look at a catalog's tempting pictures and glowing descriptions, and the call of the earth gets totally out of hand. Tomatoes, peppers, lettuce and radishes won't seem enough. Why not some eggplant? The beets look easy. Carrots take no space at all. Here's a spinach that can grow against the wall!

Such euphoria is common to almost all city gardeners when they first discover that they can grow fruits and vegetables as well as African violets. And that's part of the fun. But the available amount of space and sunlight, as well as the size of your pocketbook, are practical realities. While enjoying the catalog, think of the number of containers involved, the pounds (perhaps tons) of soil to be moved and the hours of care your plants will require.

Farm whatever space you have, but don't go beyond what it and you can reasonably produce. Resist the temptation to plant too many seeds of the same crop (unless you plan to give away the extra seedlings—and they do make nice gifts). And be careful not to plant too many kinds of crops in any one year. One fruit-laden tomato plant, a thriving green pepper and a mint-condition container or two of lettuce and radishes are far more rewarding than ten assorted pots of this and that, all in various stages of anemia and struggling for survival. After all, there's always another spring.

So be selective—think big but start small. Try anything that tempts your palate. The nicest part of gardening is that you can become an "expert" in the time it takes to bring a plant from seed to the supper table.

WHAT CAN YOU GROW?

Tomatoes

Of all the grow-your-own crops, tomatoes are the most rewarding. For the space they take, they pay handsome dividends, not only in the amount of fruit produced (continuously over a long season), but also in quality. Vine-ripened fruits make the market offering seem unpalatable. Wait till you taste your first home-grown crop.

Since seedlings of the tomato varieties best suited for container gardening are not widely available in local stores, plan on starting plants from seed. Shop the catalogs and order early enough so that the seeds can be started at least six to eight weeks in advance of the last predicted frost. (The seed packet will sometimes give outdoor planting dates by geographic zones. If it doesn't, call the local Weather Service for your area's average frost-free date.) Find the date for the zone in which you live, then count back eight weeks to determine when to sow seeds indoors. For best results, sow in individual peat pots and transplant later to permanent containers. Wait until the weather is dependably warm before putting the seedlings out. Remember to accustom them gradually to outdoor living, particularly if they have been raised under artificial light.

Most tomato plants will need to be staked; even the miniatures benefit from a small stake to provide support when the plant reaches full size and is bearing fruit. Insert the stake in the soil about two inches from the stem when the plant is moved to its permanent container. Otherwise you may disturb or damage the roots. You can also use a trellis or railing for support, or, with the larger plants, even try espalier (training them horizontally against an upright flat surface). When tying plants to stakes and railings, use strips of soft cloth rags or old nylon stockings—string or cord will cut into the stalk.

Tomatoes need warm temperatures to mature and produce. See that they have full sun, but protect them from scorching heat and wind. They also require a great deal of water throughout the bearing season.

Steady, continuous growth is the key to delicious and abundant fruit, co make sure that the plants have adequate food. Fertilize the seedlings at transplanting time, again in three weeks and then about once a week while they are producing fruit. Buy one of the fertilizers especially formulated for tomatoes. They provide the proper amount of phosphorus needed for setting fruit without having so much nitrogen that most of the plant's growth would to go to vine.

Tomatoes raised on a window sill or in a sheltered location may need a substitute for the bees and breeze that accomplish pollination. Otherwise, the plants may bloom prolifically but set no fruit. Each day while the plants are in blossom, give them a gentle shake to distribute the pollen. And remember that new blossoms will be opening each day over quite a long period of time. Turn plants often to keep them from growing lopsided.

Extremes in temperature may also cause blossoms to drop without setting fruit. Watch out for night temperatures below 55° and above 68° and day temperatures above 95°. Make sure to move the plants to shelter on cold nights and to shade them on very hot days.

Hormone-type sprays can also be used to help the blossoms from falling before they set fruit. These sprays, available in aerosols that produce a fine mist, are effective when blossoms drop due to cold nights, but will not help when blossoms drop due to high temperature.

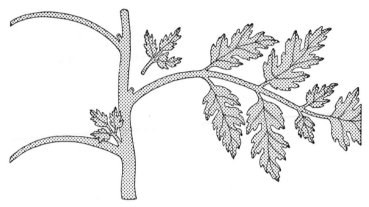

As the plants grow, you will want to prune them somewhat by taking off the first two or three "suckers" as they form. Suckers are the little shoots that appear between the main stem and the branches. Pinch or snip them out. There are different schools of thought on tomato pruning—one says that tomatoes are better off pruned to a single main stem; another maintains that it is best to let the plant develop several stems.

The city farmer must consider the particular environment his plants will have. If they are to be in full sun where reflected heat is also a factor, it may be better not to prune the plants, at least not any more than the first two or three suckers. The other suckers can then form secondary stems and the extra foliage will provide more shade for the fruit. But if the plant will not be exposed to direct, searing sunlight, then pruning to a single stem by removing all the suckers as they appear will open up the plant to more light. (If you have more than one pot of tomatoes, don't crowd them together.)

Depending on the variety, you may expect your first tomato about three to four months after planting the seeds. With proper care (light, water, food, air), the vines will continue to produce right through the fall. If the plants still have green tomatoes on them when frost threatens, bring them indoors. The tomatoes will ripen on the vine inside, even though the plant itself may have yellowed and withered leaves.

If the vines are a bit too scraggly to be passed off as potted plants, pull them up by the roots, and, if you can find a cool out-of-the-way place, hang them upside down over a line—the fruit will ripen from the energy and moisture stored in the vine. A basement is a good place—light is not especially required; an apartment storage room would work, if not too close to the furnace; or they can even be strung up in a cool part of the apartment, if you don't mind visitors' stares.

The choice of varieties for container gardening includes miniature plants that produce miniature fruits, cherry tomato types and plants that are adaptable to container growing but which bear fruits of medium size.

Maturity dates for tomatoes shown here and in catalogs usually indicate time from "setting out," or transplanting, to first fruit. Allow six to eight weeks for seeds to germinate and reach transplant stage.

🐌 **Burpee's Pixie Hybrid.** Especially developed for growing in containers. Only 14 to 18 inches tall; bears fruit larger than cherry tomato size; takes about 52 days to first fruit. A fine choice for a sunny winter window sill. Also available in a kit—pot, seed and all.

❦ **Tiny Tim.** True miniature in size and fruit (about ¾ inch in diameter); plants grow only about 15 inches tall and 14 inches across; suitable for a pot or a sunny window box; ornamental as well as a good producer, it takes about 55 days to bright red fruit.

❦ **Patio.** Developed especially for growing in tubs and containers; reaches a height of 24 to 30 inches; fruit is of medium size, red, round, of excellent quality and flavor; takes 70 days to fruit.

❦ **Tomato Stakeless.** Not specifically developed for container, but does well. Grows to height of 18 to 24 inches; takes about 80 days to fruit. The plant itself has thick, heavy, compact foliage. Fruit can average as much as 5 ounces when container-grown.

❦ **Sweet 100.** You will have lots of red, cherry-size fruit from this enormously popular tomato (the reason "100" is part of its name). Tomatoes are borne on long branches; takes about 65 to 70 days until first fruits mature. Especially sweet-tasting and an outstanding performer in a container.

❦ **Epoch.** A small-space, dwarf or bush tomato that bears larger fruit than the cherry or salad-size varieties. Bushy plant does well in a container; 80 days.

Basket King Hybrid. Bred especially for hanging baskets, window boxes, other containers. Sturdy branches cascade over the sides of the pot with clusters of fruit nearly 2 inches in diameter, round and thin-skinned; about 55 days.

Presto. These are the larger, salad-size tomatoes on container-size vines. (Fruit diameter about the size of a half-dollar.) Plants produce early and over a long period; fruit has delicious taste. Just two months to tomatoes.

Patio Prize. Another good choice for container growing; medium-size fruit on heavy, attractive foliage, takes 67 days.

Spring Giant Hybrid. Try this biggie in a large container; All-America selection (a designation for best plants introduced in any given year, as determined by judges all across the country) produces big, smooth, deep red tomatoes; bush-type vine; begins bearing in 68 days.

Peppers

Peppers are one of the most attractive crops a city gardener can grow. The sturdy plants are upright and symmetrically shaped, with dark green foliage. After the plant begins bearing, you will have blossoms and fruit in all stages of maturity throughout the summer months.

You could specialize and grow nothing but peppers and still have an enormously attractive, versatile garden. You can choose from sweet and hot; shiny reds, brilliant greens, golden yellows; cayenne, pimiento,

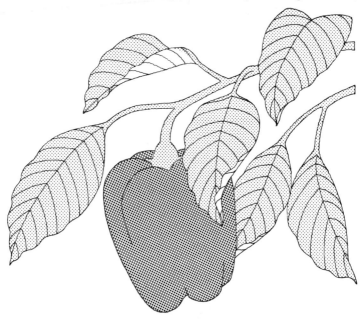

paprika, jalapeño. And the hot types aren't just red, and the mild types aren't just green. String your harvest with a needle and thread.

Sow the seed in individual peat pots (as described on page 38) for best results, and transplant later— about eight weeks or so—into permanent containers. Peppers require a long, warm growing season and about the same cultural requirements as tomatoes and eggplant. These three crops, in fact, make an eye-catching trio and are among the most productive crops you can grow—they can even make a small dent in the grocery bill.

Depending somewhat on the variety, you can harvest your first peppers about eight weeks after transplanting. And peppers needn't be full size for harvesting. Pick some of the smaller sweet peppers for use in salads while letting others reach full growth for stuffing and baking. Frequent picking will encourage production throughout the summer.

Like tomatoes, peppers can be brought in at the approach of frost. They will do quite nicely as houseplants in a sunny window, and all but the smallest fruit will finish out to maturity. The plant can also be pruned to keep it compact and carried over to the next year.

As with tomatoes, the number of days to maturity refers to average time from seedling stage to first fruit. For peppers, allow seven to eight weeks from seed to transplant stage.

❧ **Bell Boy Hybrid.** All-America selection. Plants grow 18 to 24 inches; takes about 70 days to fruit. Fruit groups near the crown of the plant, making it a good show-off for a crop in a pot. Fruit is sweet and mild; good for picking and eating on the spot.

❧ **Canape.** Early producer (only 62 days from transplanting to fruit); average-size fruit is 2 by 3 inches, sweet and mild; ripens to a brilliant red. A dozen or more fruits to a plant. Plant grows to a height of 20 to 25 inches.

ﭏ **Sweet Banana.** A lovely, ornamental plant. The long, pointed fruit appears as light green, turning yellow, then orange and finally to red as it matures. Looks like a hot pepper type but surprises you with a mild, sweet taste. Compact plant bears lots of fruit; takes about 65 days to fruit.

ﭏ **Hybrid Early Bellringer.** A sturdy, bush-type plant that produces sweet bell peppers in 60 days; keeps on bearing all summer.

ﭏ **Park's Tequila Sunrise.** Beautiful ornamental plant growing only 12 to 14 inches high. Its 4- to 5-inch-long, tapered fruits grow upright on the plant, turning to warm golden orange as they ripen; about 70 days to first fruit.

ﭏ **Park's Pot.** Plants just 10 to 12 inches high are perfect for container growing, bear lots of medium-size fruit in 45 days.

ﭏ **Pimiento.** Very thick-fleshed, mild and sweet. Fruit turns from green to a deep, glossy red. Smooth-skinned, heart-shaped pimiento pepper, averages 3½ inches in length. Let these go all the way to red and roast them for a special treat; around 75 to 80 days.

Hot Hungarian Yellow Wax. Lots of bright, canary yellow, slender, tapering fruit, 5 to 6 inches in length, on this small bush pepper. Medium hot fruit turns to crimson red when fully mature in 70 days.

Jalapeño. Favorite hot pepper for Mexican dishes. A deep, dark green when young, red when mature. Each plant bears 30 to 40 peppers in about 70 days; very hot.

Red Cherry Small. A very hot, very attractive pepper, small and nearly round, ¾ to 1¼ inches in diameter. Two-foot-high plant; bears nearly continuously after 80 days.

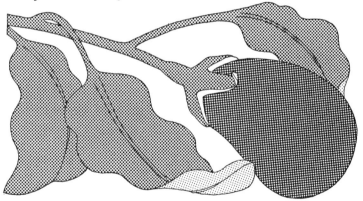

Eggplant

Eggplant is a joy to grow. The plant is as beautiful as its fruit. Its culture is similiar to that of tomatoes and green peppers. Plants require a long, warm growing season and should not be put outside until the weather is dependably warm. Eggplant seedlings are available in many garden supply houses at the same time of year (usually March or April) as tomato and green pepper plants. If you purchase seedlings, one or two (except for the midget variety) should be sufficient to produce all the fruit you are likely to use.

If you decide to raise plants from seed, do not be intimidated by reports of difficulty in germination or transplanting. Eggplants are just as easy to work with as tomatoes and are handled in the same manner. Plant seeds eight to nine weeks before it's time to put seedlings outside.

Depending upon the variety, the plants will grow from 2 to 3 feet in diameter and be bushy or flat as trained. They will begin to bear approximately 75 days after transplanting. Maturity dates for eggplant listed in catalogs usually indicate transplant time. Allow eight to nine weeks for seeds to germinate and reach transplant stage. As the blossoms appear (they are an attractive lavender), pinch off a few to keep the eggplant from setting too many fruits; about five or six per plant is best. Terminal growths on the stems can also be pinched back to maintain the shape of the plant—short and bushy or taller, as desired.

Don't wait too long to harvest. You can use the fruit any time after it is about half-grown. Don't wait until it overripens and loses its glossy shine. Not only will the fruit have a tough texture and a slightly bitter taste—the plant will stop producing.

᠘᠕ **Morden Midget (Park).** Short, sturdy, bushy plants; small-size fruit—enough for one person as a main dish, for two as an accompaniment; excellent quality; the lustrous fruit nestling in gray-green foliage makes a striking patio or porch accent. Takes 65 days.

᠘᠕ **Black Beauty.** Longtime favorite of home gardeners; produces large, traditional-size purplish-black fruit; plants grow into compact bushes and are very productive; takes 73 days from setting out of plants to maturity. Fruit will not be as large when container-grown as what you are accustomed to seeing in the market, so be sure to pick while still glossy.

᠘᠕ **Easter Egg Hybrid.** You guessed it: small, egg-shaped, pure white fruit from this unique plant. Its size (under 2 feet high) makes it a good candidate for container gardening; small fruit (in 65 days) is fun to grow and good to eat. Produces blossoms and fruit through the season.

See Oriental Vegetables for more eggplant.

Lettuce

If you can't wait to taste, grow some lettuce. Of the three general types—crisphead, butterhead and loosehead (or leaf)—the leaf varieties are best for container gardening. They require a much shorter growing sea-

son than the solid-head varieties (40 to 50 days as compared with 70 to 80 days) and are easier to grow. Leaf lettuce also makes a most attractive pot plant, producing a beautiful array of greens with interesting shapes and textures. Or plant it as a border for another container plant. Try a ring around your fruit tree in early spring.

Leaf lettuce needs no transplanting. The seed can be sown very early in the spring directly into the container or area where it is to mature. A light frost will not kill it, though it may slow growth. The lettuce produces "instant" crops. You can be eating its "thinnings" in about three weeks. Successive plantings made at 10-day intervals will supply tender thinnings for weeks. As the lettuce matures, choose mostly outer leaves along with a few of the inner ones each cutting. You won't believe the flavor of lettuce eaten the same day it's picked.

Usually, after about two months' growth, the leaves begin to toughen and the plants go quickly to seed. At this point, discard the plant entirely or keep it watered and cared for till the cool fall weather when it will reseed itself and produce a new crop of tender leaves. Remember, lettuce just can't take heat.

Salad Bowl. Frilly, curled leaves with long stems; resembles chicory or curly endive, but is light green; leaves are crisp and tender; grows high, wide and handsome in its container; 48 days to mature.

Oak Leaf. Small-leaved, deep, compact plant; more heat-resistant than most varieties; not as frilly as other leaf lettuce, it forms more of a rosette and is extremely attractive; matures in about 40 days.

Black-Seeded Simpson. Inner leaves of Simpson are almost white, outer leaves are broad and wavy and frilled at the edges; available in preplanted kits as well as seed packets; matures in about 45 days.

Ruby. A conversation piece as well as good eating—bright green leaves are tinged with red; takes about 47 days from seed to fruit.

Tom Thumb. A miniature butterhead-type that is actually a cross between a butterhead and crisphead; matures in about two months; produces small, rosette-shaped plants; use whole for individual salad servings.

Buttercrunch. All-American bibb-type; thick and crunchy leaves, loosely folded to the heart, with a wonderfully delicate flavor; easy to grow; broad, dark green leaves in 75 days.

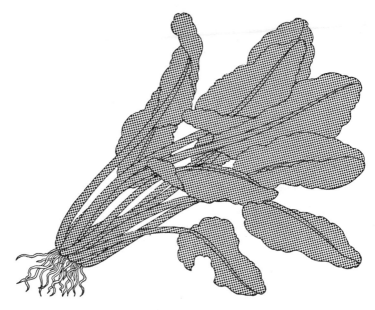

Spinach

No one's indifferent toward spinach. You either like it (raw or cooked) or you don't. But even those who hate it on a plate will love it on a patio—spinach makes a beautiful foliage plant, with leaves of varied textures and dark green color. It is a cool-season crop and should be planted in early spring or late summer. Where winters are mild, seed can be sown in the fall, overwintered and produced as an early crop in the spring. Plan on a single plant for each 8- to 10-inch pot, and be sure to leave room for several pots. Seed can be sown indoors in individual peat pots and transplanted to permanent containers later; or it can be sown directly into the permanent container.

For best flavor, spinach should be grown fast (use a fertilizer high in nitrogen). When harvesting, thin out leaves from each plant to keep the containers balanced and to encourage growth of the remaining plants.

Like other leaf crops, spinach needs plenty of water. It cannot take heat at all (over 80° is too hot), so if you want to grow greens through the summer, substitute Swiss chard for spinach.

Swiss chard is not discouraged by hot weather; the leaves are large and crinkly and grow on long white or crimson stalks. Plant as for spinach, water generously, harvest the outer leaves only and it will produce through the summer.

Bloomsdale. Old-fashioned variety that forms a rosette of crinkled, glossy, dark green leaves; looks great in a container and tastes and looks great on the table; 48 days from seed to salad.

Winter Bloomsdale. A rugged variety that takes cold weather; approximately 45 days.

New Zealand Spinach. Not a true spinach, but popular because it can take hot weather when regular spinach would bolt or become bitter. Thick, fleshy triangular leaves. Pick only the growing tips and you will have a continuous crop from early summer to late fall. Takes 70 days from seed.

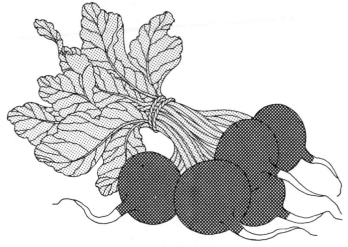

Radishes

Radishes are foolproof and fast for window sill, porch or patio. Sow the seeds in the container in which they will grow. Radishes must be grown fast— fertilize them at planting time and plan on a crop within three to four weeks. Give plants plenty of water to make them crisp and tender. Don't sow seeds too thickly and be sure to thin them out to at least an inch apart so that each radish will have room to develop. Radishes do well in artificial soil because the developing roots can expand easily in the light-textured soil.

Sow seeds early, as the plants cannot make it

through the hot weather. A light frost will not hurt them. If you plan on more than one container, sow seeds a week or so apart so that they won't all mature at once. They must be eaten when mature or they turn pithy.

You can get two crops out of one container by a sort of reforestation plan—when you pull each radish, replace it with another seed. Also, harvest every other radish to keep the foliage nicely balanced in the container. The foliage is decorative, producing something between a rosette and fountain effect. Try them around the rim of a large container, circling a planting of green onions.

Cherry Belle. Popular round, smooth, red radish; crisp and tender; short tops make them good choice for container growing; just 24 days from seed to table.

Champion. A former All-America selection; bright red; round shape; matures in 24 days.

White Icicle. Pure white, root-shaped like its namesake; 6 inches long; mild, sweet and juicy; matures in 27 days.

China Rose. A fall and winter radish; plant in midsummer. Rosy radish fades to a light pink near the tip of the root; about 50 days to harvest. Crisp white inside with a very pungent taste. You'll know you've eaten a radish.

German Giant. Big as turnips; crisp, white flesh. Serve them peeled round and round in curls for eating raw à la German beer gardens. Good with cocktails, too. Takes 29 days.

See Oriental Vegetables for more radishes.

Onions

Most gardeners who grow onions like to start with either "sets" or with very young plants instead of seed. Sets are small, dry bulbs that can be bought by weight. Each one will produce a full-size onion. Half a pound (1 pint) of sets will cost about $3 and contain 75 to 100 bulbs. The young plants are sold in bunches of 75 for about $3 at local garden shops or nurseries. They are usually slightly higher if ordered from a catalog.

If you plan to harvest your crop as green onions (scallions), white sets and plants are preferable to yellow. Plant the sets or plants about an inch apart and an inch deep. Green onions from plants will be ready to eat in about three weeks; sets will take about five weeks. Harvest every other one so the remaining onions will have room to develop larger bulbs. With loose soil and regular feeding, they grow big and fat.

If you are growing green onions from seed, Evergreen White Bunching seed is recommended. Each of these seeds sends up several shoots. You can pile soil around the shoot as it grows to keep it blanched white. These onions do not form bulbs. They require about four months from planting time to scallion size, although you can use them for flavoring within two months.

Onions can be planted very early in the spring. A light frost will not harm them; they enjoy full sun.

Shallots

Shallots are expensive to buy, so grow your own for a treat. They are produced in clusters from a set. Their delicate flavor makes them welcome anywhere an onion flavor is the least bit too strong—in salads, scrambled eggs and omelets, and with mushrooms. For some wonderful, yet simple, French recipes, only shallots will do.

Shallots are easy to grow and they are not hurt by frost, so you can start them both early and late in the year. There are two types, red- and yellow-skinned. The yellow are a little larger; otherwise there is not much difference between them. You should have firm bulbs of medium size. Place bulbs in the soil with the top third of the pointed end showing. As the bulb takes root the tip will turn green. Each bulb, as it grows, will split up to form a cluster of new bulbs. As the plant matures, in about four months, the tops will turn yellow and flop over. Dig around the plant and pull out the clusters along with the tops. Leave them to dry; do not split clusters apart yet or remove tops. After the tops have withered and the bulbs have dried, break up the clusters, rub off any loose skins, and store in the refrigerator.

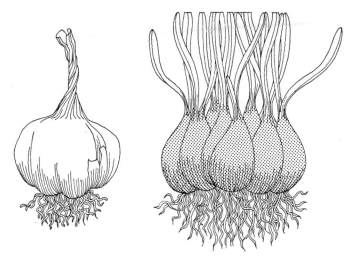

Garlic

Garlic is easy and pretty to grow. Buy a garlic bulb at a grocery or garden store. Break the cloves apart and plant them a couple of inches apart in a container. Make holes the depth of the clove and insert them, pointed end up. Garlic grows best in cool weather, so if growing indoors, keep in the coolest window. You can start garlic outside as soon as danger of hard frost is past. In a protected corner, garlic doesn't mind the cold.

The onionlike tops grow fast in cool fall and spring

weather, and then at a certain point, growth shifts to the bulb. Keep the plant continuously moist. It is ready to harvest when the tops fall over and turn yellow. Pull the bulbs up just before the tops have dried out completely, and you can braid them, along with the bulbs, into a string of garlic.

One clove of elephant garlic is about 10 times the size of a clove of true garlic, and its flavor is milder and sweeter. (The name comes from its large size.) Plant cloves an inch deep; will not grow as big if planted deeper. Plants grow 30 to 36 inches tall. Hold off on watering when tops start to turn yellow and wither. Wait to harvest until tops are yellowed.

Carrots

Since carrots are always available in groceries, many city farmers discount them as a possible container crop. However, one taste of a tender baby carrot—2 to 3 inches long and ½ inch in diameter—can be a whole new carrot experience, one worth savoring. Carrots are easy to grow and their fresh sweetness and crunchy texture are reward enough for the container space.

Artificial soil really comes into its own in raising carrots. Light, loose and free of lumps, it permits the rapid growth that carrots must have to be tender and sweet.

Carrot seed should be sown directly into its permanent containers. Make sure to coordinate the container with the variety of carrot grown, since carrot length will vary all the way from the 3-inch Tiny Sweet to the 6-inch Nantes. Obviously, you will need a planter deep enough to accommodate the length of the variety (or the length to which you will let it grow before harvesting), plus a couple of inches to spare. If your container is not deep enough, the carrot roots may just turn sideways and keep on growing, with underground chaos the result.

Seed can be sown in spring (up until very warm weather, actually) or fall. The soil needs to be kept moist during the germination period, which is sometimes as long as two or even three weeks. So it is a good idea, after sowing the seed in damp soil, to cover the top of the container with a sheet of plastic wrapping until the seeds sprout. Then remove the wrapping and water with a fine mist- or sprinkler-type can, as needed.

When the seedlings are about 2 inches tall, thin them to about an inch apart. An application of fertilizer at this time will help spur the fast growth essential for tender, juicy carrots. About four weeks later, the little baby carrots will have formed; thin the plants again to about 3 inches apart. This time, though, pull some to eat. The fresh flavor of these tender "thinnings" is a delightful taste treat; while you enjoy the early harvest, you will be giving the remainder of the plants room to develop to full maturity. Give the feathery foliage an occasional misting during hot weather. Most varieties require 65 to 75 days to mature to full size.

Tiny Sweet. Midget variety; roots grow to 3 inches; ready to eat in two months; tender and crisp.

Short'n Sweet. Grows 3½ to 4 inches long and about 2 inches thick at the top; 68 days to mature.

Nantes Coreless. Matures to about 6 inches in 68 days; smooth, well-flavored carrot with practically no visible core.

Little Finger. A baby carrot, only about ½ inch round and 3 inches long; matures in about 65 days. Tuck about 15 seeds into an 8-inch-wide pot. Small tops mean more room in the pot for more plants. A gourmet treat cooked and served whole.

Gold Nugget. A chunky little carrot, more round than long (2 to 3 inches); matures in about 71 days. Crisp, sweet eating; great for relish trays.

Mini Express. You will have small, slim carrots, 3½ to 4 inches long, smooth-skinned and nearly coreless, tender and sweet, in about 65 days.

Early French Fame. This is a European variety; only 2 inches long, good-tasting with a smooth, deep orange-red color. Takes about 67 days.

☙ **Royal Chantenay.** Broad, blocky shape, orange color all the way through. Harvest small or full-grown; good flavor either way. Matures in about 70 days.

☙ **Nantes Half Long.** Perfectly cylindrical, 6 to 7 inches long with same thickness the whole length. Attractive to serve, cooked or raw, sliced in rounds. About 70 days.

Beets

Beets are a practical container crop because the plant is completely edible. The beets themselves will be deliciously sweet and the tops can be used for salads or cooked greens.

Beet seeds are actually small balls (fruits) containing several seeds. Soak seeds overnight for faster germination. Once planted, several seedlings emerge in a bunch. When the plants have grown to a height of 2 inches, they should be thinned to stand about 1½ inches apart. After they reach about 8 inches, they should be thinned again. Use thinnings in soups, salads, sandwiches, stir-fry dishes. Remove every other plant, leaving a 3-inch space between plants. Don't let the beets themselves grow too large before final harvesting. Their flavor is best when they are young. Pull the vegetables when they are about 1½ inches in diameter.

Beets prefer cool temperatures; sow early in the

spring or in the fall. They have a way of heaving out of the soil as they grow; when they do, simply put a bit more earth on top to cover them.

The plants will do well in artificial soil. Their seedlings are small and weak and benefit from the fine texture of artificial soil; clods of real dirt interfere with the developing root. Choose containers at least 8 to 10 inches deep.

ﻬ **Ruby Queen.** Dark green tops are short (10 to 12 inches) and make attractive pot plants; the root is round, smooth and bright red; sweet flavor and fine texture make tender, delicious eating—pickled or cooked; matures in about 55 days.

ﻬ **Detroit Dark Red.** Produces a deep, dark red root, and crimson color also shows in the leaves; sweet-flavored and tender; good for greens, too; takes about 58 days to mature.

ﻬ **Burpee's Golden Beet.** Has reddish, golden roots; tops make delicious boiled greens, very nutritious. Beets are best eaten small, but retain tenderness and sweet flavor even when larger. Matures in about 55 days; definitely unique.

ﻬ **Little Ball.** Grows quickly (50 days) so you can plant a crop in early spring and again in late summer. Plant close together—10 or 12 seeds to an 8-inch-wide pot. Harvest small round beets and plant again.

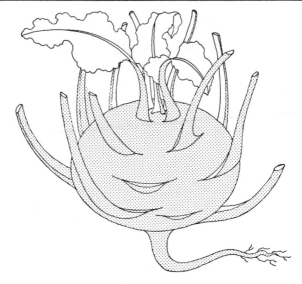

Kohlrabi

The name of this fascinating plant comes from the German words *Kohl* (cabbage) and *Rabi* (turnip). It looks more like an aboveground green turnip than like a cabbage; it also has a nutty, turniplike, but milder flavor. The bulb is not a root, like the turnip, but rather the swollen stem of the plant which bulges out at ground level as the plant matures. Tall, slender stalks grow from the bulb. Atop the stems are its small, cabbagelike leaves. Kohlrabi is best tasting when about 1½ to 2 inches in diameter. Use in stir-fry Chinese dishes, substitute for turnips, or peel and serve raw as a dipper and for munching. Kohlrabi is as easy to grow as a radish. Seed ½ inch deep. It needs to grow fast, so feed and water well. The plant's sparse top growth will not shade nearby crops—onions or beets make a good combination. Bulbs mature quickly. Cut an inch below stem to harvest. Hybrid Grand Duke and Early White Vienna are widely available varieties. Harvest 50 to 55 days after sowing.

Bush Beans

Bush beans—all kinds—are the best bean bet for container gardening. (Pole beans are more productive, but not as attractive.) The low-growing bush beans can be lined up in a row for a sort of "edible hedge" or stationed about the patio to pose as shrubs. The mature plants will be 1 to 2 feet high, depending on the variety.

Plan several pots if you have the space. You will dress up the patio and be able to harvest enough young beans at one time for a meal. Eight to ten bean bushes should supply a small family for several weeks. Most varieties will provide five or six pickings over the season. Pick the beans while they are young—before the seeds begin to swell in the pod. Early harvest not only ensures good flavor but also encourages productivity.

Lima beans do best in regions with a long growing season. If this poses a problem, choose the small butter bean which requires less growing time. These beans also need warm weather. They will respond to lots of water and to fertilizer, especially when the pods begin to form. Give the seeds a head start by soaking them overnight in warm water before planting. Sow seeds in early spring, directly into the container in which they are to mature, spacing them as indicated on the seed packet.

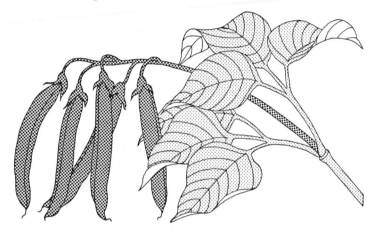

Look for bush versions of the Italian Romano pole bean that is so popular in southern Europe. Properly cooked (which means quickly) and with a light butter or oil seasoning, these broad, flat-podded beans are among the best beans you can eat.

Fava beans are a favorite in Europe, where they are also known as faba, English dwarf, shell or broad beans. Their taste is something of a cross between a pea and a lima bean, only better. They can be eaten at a very early stage, like snap beans or green peas, but the older, shelled beans are unbeatable when simmered or stewed. These beans like cool weather and need lots of moisture. The standard varieties require four to five months to mature, but dwarf varieties that mature faster are available.

🫘 Provider Bush.

Compact plant produces lots of straight, tender pods, 5 to 6 inches long. Experiment with a container to see if you like the unusually robust taste. Harvest the beans in 50 days; try them frenched and raw in salads, for the kind of crunch you get from sprouts.

🫘 Henderson Bush Lima.

An old favorite; produces lots of tender, sweet beans; pick when young; each pod yields 3 to 4 small, flat green beans; 65 days from seed to maturity.

🫘 Royal Burgundy Purple Pod.

New, hardier version of old favorite; lovely plants produce dark, round purple pods, which turn green after cooking two minutes. Delicious, tender, stringless and beautiful—a great combination for the container gardener; takes 50 to 55 days to mature.

🫘 Roma.

A bush Romano with a distinctive taste; smooth, succulent pods 5 inches long. Plant three to a 10- or 12-inch pot; matures in about 55 days.

🫘 Jumbo Romano.

Large, flat, good-tasting pods on a bush plant in about 55 days. Beans can grow a foot long, but should be picked earlier for good eating and to keep plants bearing.

Bush Fava Bean Long Pod. True upright bushes, large but heavy-yielding. Inedible pods, 7 inches long, hold 5 to 7 big, flat, light green beans. Plant early; they hate hot weather; 85 days to maturity.

Dwarf Broad Bean. Plant branches naturally to make several stems. Plan on one plant to a 10-inch pot. After the first pods begin to form, pinch the growing tips of the plant to turn its energy to pod production. Begin picking when beans inside pod are about ½ inch across; 85 days.

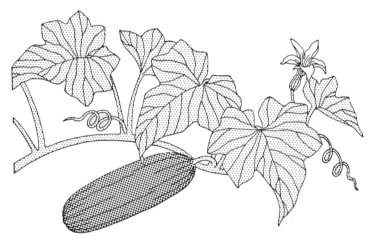

Cucumbers

Gardeners who are still a bit timid in the presence of tiny, frail sprouts will welcome cucumbers and their sturdy, robust, aggressive seedlings. Cucumbers make a strong statement from the minute they pop up.

Cucumbers may be sown indoors in peat pots very early in the spring and transplanted to the permanent container outdoors after all danger of frost has passed. Or they may be sown indoors directly into the permanent container. The use of small, individual peat pots merely allows you to handle more seedlings in a small area.

If you sow directly into the permanent container, plant in "hills"—several seeds planted together. Plant 6 to 8 seeds in the middle of a large container (and later thin 3 or 4 plants) for a generous display of vine and fruit.

The vines will trail unless trained. Put a piece of fencing in, or next to, the planter; or set the planter next to a railing or trellis. Train the vine early before fruit begins to set. If you're late in positioning the vines, you may expose the developing fruits to too much direct sun and they will shrivel and die.

Cucumbers left to develop normally will seek the protective shade of the leaves. In training the vine, allow the center stem to grow as high as the fence, railing or trellis. Pinch it off to allow the lateral stems to develop, and then train these sideways.

Cucumbers also do well in hanging baskets. The vines can be allowed to trail to the floor or trained to a nearby trellis or railing. Remember, however, that cucumber tendrils will entwine around whatever they can reach, including a nearby plant—so use a string or cord of some kind to train them away from their neighbors. The plants take from 55 to 70 days to mature, depending on the variety and your taste. If you're partial to tiny, sweet pickles, harvest in about 40 days. If you prefer them sliced in salads or as bread-and-butter pickles, just leave them on the vine until they reach the right size. The plants will continue to produce until frost, but will slow down and not bear at all during very hot weather.

Patio Pik. A compact, dwarf plant adapted to container growing, with fruit that sets early; takes about 51 days from seed to maturity. Medium green color, fruit grows 4 to 6 inches long.

Spacemaster Bush. With its short vines and no runners, this variety is great for small spaces. The 8-inch-long fruit has a good, crisp taste; 60 days.

Pot Luck Hybrid. Developed especially for small-garden and container growing. Vines grow only about 18 inches long, but produce lots of 6- to 8-inch, straight, dark green fruit in 58 days.

Bush Crop. Small bushy vine; spread 2½ to 3 feet across. Although plants are small for a cucumber, they yield a big crop of crisp-tasting cucumbers in 60 days.

Cucumber Bush Whopper. Dwarf, rounded plants well-suited to container; good yields of 6- to 8-inch-long, crisp, good-tasting cucumbers in 55 days.

See Oriental Vegetables for more cucumbers.

Squash

Like its relative the cucumber, the summer squash produces a great deal of fruit (on bushy, compact plants) and grows rapidly enough for even the most impatient gardener. Actually, you must be on your toes at harvest time; fruits will outgrow their prime for eating in a matter of a few days.

If all of your harvest is destined for the dinner table, resist the temptation to see how large the fruit will grow. They may double in size after their prime. Since most farmers enjoy boasting about the size of the fruit they produce as well as quantity and quality, you might want to let a couple of squash go the limit, but for the best eating, harvest while young—as soon as the skin can be pierced by the fingernail with almost no pressure. Keep the fruit picked in order to keep the vine producing.

Zucchini can be harvested when fruits are only about 2 inches long and about ½ inch in diameter. These are delicious cubed and sautéed in butter. At 3 to 5 inches long they are good baked; larger still but not overmature fruits are marvelous sliced and fried.

Since squash is a member of the cucumber family, planting and culture are similar. Seeds can be planted indoors, early in the spring in individual peat pots, or outdoors, in permanent containers after all danger of frost has passed. If sown outdoors, plant 5 or 6 seeds to a hill and thin to the 3 or 4 strongest-looking seedlings. Apply soluble fertilizer when the plants are about 4 inches tall.

The permanent container for squash should be as large as you can manage—a bushel basket or washtub, for example. Give the squash as much sun as possible—moving the containers about as needed. Squash roots should be kept moist almost continually, so mulch the top of the container with peat or sphagnum moss or shredded newspapers.

Winter squash grows as a vine and, if left untrimmed, can overrun your balcony. Snip it back judiciously, sacrificing some of the crop to make room for other vegetables and for yourself. The fruit ripens in the fall and most recommendations (unlike those for summer squash) call for leaving the fruit on the vine until it is fully mature and the rind hardened. Actually, this is to allow the grower to store the squash through the winter because the fruit will not keep unless it is well-matured. The fruit can, however, be eaten before it reaches maturity. The flavor is good, although different from that of mature fruit.

Summer Squash

🐌 **Green Magic.** Space-saving, 18-inch dwarf plant bears lots of dark green, 6- to 8-inch zucchini. Starts bearing 48 days from seed.

🐌 **Gourmet Globe.** Beautiful new round-type zucchini; open bush plants save space; pick fruit when 4 inches across; about 50 days.

🐌 **Peter Pan.** Compact bush plants produce this pretty, green-tinted scalloped squash in 45 days; harvest when no more than 3 inches across.

🐌 **Tara.** Bush vine is smaller than other crooknecks. Rich golden yellow fruit, their oval bulbs tapering to a slim, crooked neck. Pick when 3 to 4 inches long; takes about 51 days.

🐌 **Jersey Golden Acorn.** This plant makes a double hit as a summer–winter squash. An All-America selection, designed by the breeder in bush form and producing lovely golden acorn fruit. Plant grows 4 to 5 feet across, relatively small for squash. Any runners that appear can be snipped off. Fruit picked early (about the size of a golf ball) can be used as yellow summer squash, others can be left on the plant for nearly six weeks to be used as a winter squash. About 50 days to eat as summer squash; 80 to 90 days to maturity and for storing.

Fall and Winter Squash

Sweet Mama. Restricted vine growth. Produces lots of dark green, blocky, drum-shaped fruits in 84 days; a good squash pick for a container.

Bush Buttercup. Rich, sweet flavor, deep orange flesh, and not stringy. Dark green fruit in 100 days.

Gold Nugget. Round, bright orange fruit, enormous leaves and beautiful yellow flowers; bushlike growth habits make it excellent for containers; matures in about 95 days.

Bush Table King. An All-America selection. Acorn type; fruits are 5 inches in diameter; dark green skin with pale orange flesh; delicious when baked; takes 85 days from seed to maturity.

Herbs

Interest in gourmet cooking has zoomed in recent years; not far behind is the gourmet gardener, growing his own herbs and snipping off leaves and stems at their peak of quality and flavor Do-it-yourself kits now make herbs the easiest possible gardening project for an apartment resident. A selection of seeds, the pots and planting mix are all put together in one package. Such kits are widely available in specialty shops, department stores and gift catalogs, as well as from the usual seed sources.

A typical kit might contain 12 peat pots, potting soil and an assortment of seeds: basil, dill, marjoram, oregano, parsley, sage and thyme. All of these plants are relatively easy to grow, and the kit is a painless and productive introduction to herb culture.

The herbs listed above, plus many others, are also available in separate seed packets from seed companies and off the rack at garden shops. (Parsley is usually listed in the vegetable section of the catalog.) Many herbs are perennials (plants that reseed themselves and come up each year) and can grow to be old friends. Most can be overwintered indoors, if necessary, but tend to get spindly. Many will fare better if allowed to remain outdoors in a sheltered spot protected from severe cold. Almost all varieties can be dried and stored. (Keep them in tightly closed glass containers out of strong light.)

Beginners who go beyond the preplanted kits might start with seed for three annuals—dill, savory and sweet basil. All germinate quickly and can be sown where they are to grow—but sparingly. Extra plants should be pinched off at ground level. For faster germination, parsley seed should be soaked in water for 24 hours before planting. It doesn't pay to grow chives from seed; potted clumps are relatively inexpensive and often available at supermarkets.

You don't have to be a cook to be an herb fancier. Their foliage and fragrance are reward enough for the small space they take up. For a lovely aroma try lemon balm or lemon verbena, and the various mints, from spearmint to apple mint.

A strawberry jar with a variety of herbs peeking from its pockets will make an intriguing and useful "garden accompli" indoors or out. Most culinary herbs love sun, so a south or west window usually suits them best. Most also need to dry out between waterings. Gourmet gardeners who want their herbs close at hand on the kitchen counter should plan on a double row of fluorescent lights under the kitchen cabinet and place the pots of herbs so that they are up close to the lights. Flat fluorescent fixtures that fit snugly under a kitchen cabinet and that can be plugged into an outlet are widely available at hardware stores. They are relatively inexpensive and well worth the small cost and effort to provide a seasoning shelf of live herbs at your fingertips.

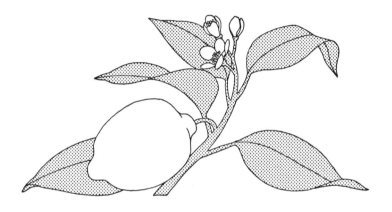

Citrus

City gardeners can have the best of both worlds, the houseplant and the edible crop, with a dwarf citrus tree. Try oranges, lemons or limes. Gorgeous foliage, fragrant blossoms, colorful and delicious fruit and limited culture requirements make citrus a favorite of almost everyone who has grown it.

Citrus trees *can* be started from seeds of fruit purchased at the grocery. However, novices often have difficulty in getting these seeds to germinate. If the seeds do sprout, the plants do not always bloom; if blooming stage is reached, fruit does not always set; and finally, if fruit does grow, it is rarely "true" to the fruit which produced the seed. Forget it! Purchase citrus plants from the garden shop or order them from a catalog. They are not expensive—around $2.50 each for one-year-old plants; $5 each for two-year-old (bearing age) plants. The year-old plants are about a foot tall; the two-year-old plants about two feet tall. They can reach a height of six or seven feet, or they can be cut back and maintained at three or four feet or even less. Once they are established, they can be in various stages of flowering and fruiting for much of the year. They will bear for years and years.

Although citrus trees can be grown successfully indoors (all the time), they do seem to appreciate being outside in mild weather; and they can certainly smarten up a balcony, porch or patio. If you like, move them outdoors in the spring after the weather is dependably warm. Follow the procedure for hardening plants by managing the shift without sudden, sharp changes in temperature and overexposure to direct sun. Don't put them out, for example, until the temperature is close to what they have been accustomed to indoors; 60° to 70° weather would be about right. For a gradual adjustment, leave them out for a few hours at a time, bringing them back in before the temperature gets too hot or drops too low. And shade them from the direct sun until they are used to it.

If you must keep a citrus tree indoors the year round, put it in your sunniest window. Rotate the tree about once a week so that all sides get exposure to the sun. This will encourage the balanced development of the tree as well as the growth of blossoms and fruit. The trees should also be kept away from radiators or heat ducts.

Citrus trees require a lot of water and should be fertilized every three to four weeks while they are bearing fruit (which is for a good part of the year). Also, give them just a pinch of chelated iron once a month. The trees prefer a humid atmosphere, so to combat the dry heat common to apartments, fill a tray with gravel, keep it wet continuously and put the citrus container on the tray. If you have more than one plant, group them together under these same conditions. The more water around to evaporate, the better.

The plants will profit from an occasional bath. Use a warm, slightly soapy cloth to carefully wipe each leaf both top and underside. This not only rids the leaves of accumulated dust that clogs their breathing apparatus, but also helps ward off scale (a major pest of citrus) and other insects. If you set the whole plant in the shower, be sure the shower head is adjusted to a fine mist, otherwise the force of the water will dislodge the soil. Let the leaves dry before putting the plant back in direct sunlight.

An added note about scale: Should you spot a sticky-looking substance on the leaves of the plant, scale is likely to be the culprit. Turn the leaf over, and if you look closely you will see one or several tiny, round, light brown "spots." This is scale. Look closely, because when the scale is attached along the main vein of the leaf it is sometimes hard to see.

A shower won't take care of this problem. Use a warm, soapy cloth and clean each leaf—gently loosening each scale as you go. The job may take a little while, but it is time well spent to keep the plant healthy. Usually the chore need not be repeated; if at all, only every few weeks.

Here are some space-saving varieties suitable for indoor "groves":

Calamondin Orange. This tree tends to grow tall and columnar; it produces an abundance of blossoms and fruit, often in different stages of maturity at the same time, for 9 to 10 months of the year. Small, waxy, green leaves; oranges develop 1 to 1½ inches in diameter.

Ponderosa Lemon. Leaves are larger than the Calamondin orange and lighter green in color; bears full-size fruit; a single lemon is often 3 to 4 inches in diameter, and weighs more than 3 pounds (one is enough for a large pie); blossoms are small, waxy and trumpet-shaped in especially fragrant clusters.

Persian Lime. Perfumed white flowers against glossy green foliage; lots of full-size, bright green fruit, summer and winter.

Ruby Red Grapefruit. Sweet pink-fleshed fruit from a small evergreen tree.

Dwarf Fruit

With the genetic dwarf trees now on the market, you can grow delectable fruit at home. These miniature trees also make lovely ornamental plants, many of them growing no more than 4 to 6 feet tall. The fruits, however, are full-size and flavorful. You can enjoy them from mid- to late summer, with the trees beginning to bear one to three years after planting and producing from 1 to 3 bushels of fruit per year.

Many of the dwarf or miniature trees are self-pollinating—that is, they do not need another tree close-by in order to bear fruit. However, some do require a second tree for pollination. Read catalog descriptions carefully so that you are aware of which trees will need a mate.

Order the trees for spring planting. They will probably be shipped in late February or early March and will arrive bare-rooted; they will also be accompanied by good, clear instructions on planting and care. (Before planting, check the sections in this book on selecting containers and preparing them for proper drainage. The potting mixture should be half garden soil and half peat moss.) Keep your tubbed tree in the shade at first, gradually moving it to full exposure. Use a mulch (a protective layer on top of the soil) of peat or sphagnum moss to help keep the soil from drying out.

The fruit trees listed here are deciduous, meaning they shed their leaves every fall and enter a dormant period until the following spring. To be productive, the tree must be exposed to a certain amount of cold. Therefore, if you live in an area where winters are very mild, your tree may never become dormant and will thus fail to produce fruit. If you live in a cold-winter area, the tree will have to be protected during periods of prolonged subfreezing temperatures. Fruit trees in containers will need to have their roots, as well as tops, protected from the cold. An ideal covering is a large cardboard carton such as those used to ship refrigerators, televisions and other large appliances. Most stores are happy to give these away. Put a thick layer of newspapers or other insulation under the container, and several layers around the sides, held in place with cord. Then just upend the carton over all.

Give the tree one last good soaking after cold weather comes but before the long, hard winter sets in. Then let it take the first freeze or so with the container part protected only by the layers of newspapers (these can be kept dry with a plastic covering, if necessary). Now, move the tree to a sheltered location (a corner of the balcony, for example), pop the carton over it and add no more water until spring. Begin watering again as soon as the soil thaws, but beware of late spring frost and do not remove the protective insulation too early.

Peaches

ટ✿⌣ **Stark Sensation.** Grows 6 to 8 feet in height with full-size, yellow-flesh, freestone peaches.

ટ✿⌣ **Garden Sun.** Large, juicy fruit on 5- to 6-foot tree, especially recommended for lower South.

Nectarines

ટ✿⌣ **Garden Delight.** Grows 5 to 6 feet tall; dark pink double blossoms in spring; followed by sweet-tasting fruit.

ટ✿⌣ **Stark Sweet Melody.** Lovely, full-size red fruit on 6- to 8-feet-high tree.

ટ✿⌣ **Dwarf Mericrest.** Firm, sweet, juicy fruit; winter hardy.

Apricots

ટ✿⌣ **Stark GoldenGlo.** Grows only 4 to 6 feet tall; produces lots of medium-sized, sweet-tasting fruit, and makes a lovely spring-flowering ornamental as well.

ટ✿⌣ **Garden Annie.** Firm, juicy, bright yellow apricots. Grows 8 to 10 feet tall.

Aprigold. Full-size apricots on compact tree that provides beautiful foliage, flowers and fruit.

Apples

Garden Delicious. Bears sweet-tasting, greenish-yellow apples on 6- to 8-foot trees.

Starkspur Compact Mac. Grows 6 to 8 feet tall with full-size McIntosh apples.

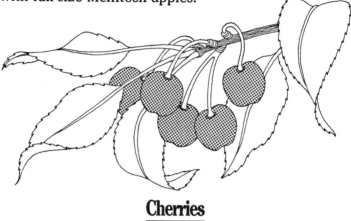

Cherries

Garden Bing. Produces light crops of sweet, dark red cherries; grows to about 6 feet.

Figs

Fig trees require only a minimum of care and will provide lots of fruit for eating and preserving. They need six to eight hours of sunlight a day, so would fare best on the patio or balcony.

They should be brought in for the winter and literally stored away. Since this is their resting period, they need very little light or water, but they should have a reasonably low temperature, certainly lower than ordinary room temperature. An unheated attic, cellar or garage is a good place; in an apartment, possibly a room set aside for the tenant's storage needs. If you have an area that you can keep on the cool side and want to try to overwinter the tree, plan to bring it in before the heat goes on.

If there is no suitable storage space and your winters are not too severe, you might try overwintering your fig tree outside. It must be sheltered from both frost and wind. Gardeners are always being told to mulch their plants with straw or hay to protect them from the cold, but in the city these products are difficult to find. Shredded newspaper will work as mulch, but it disintegrates if it gets wet. If the tree is placed under a sheltering roof where it can be kept dry, newspaper is worth a try. Cut it into strips and then crumple it together. Pack the shredded newspapers on the soil around the base of the plant up to the first limbs. Dampen the newspaper slightly to pack it more firmly around the base of the tree. A 2- or 3-inch layering of the plastic peanuts used as packing material also makes a good top covering over the newspaper mulch. In the spring, remove the mulch and resume watering to bring the plant into active growth.

🐦 **Everbearing.** Better for northern areas; very sweet fruit, perfect for eating fresh or for preserves; ripens in July or before frost begins.

🐦 **Brown Turkey.** Only for southern climates; medium-size bronze fruit, ripens in mid-July.

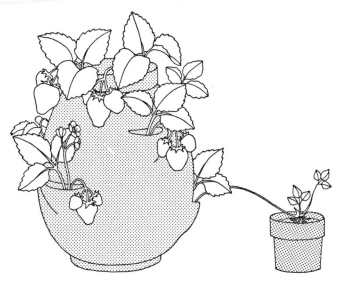

Strawberries

Strawberries provide an interesting challenge for the city gardener. The challenge is in the planting; the berries are actually easy to grow and require minimum care. New methods and equipment developed with the limited-space gardener in mind are a great aid in producing this luscious fruit.

There are two kinds of strawberries to grow: the

everbearing varieties, which produce one crop in the autumn of the year in which they are planted, and additional crops in the spring and fall of the following years; and the June-bearing varieties, which do not bear fruit until the year after planting. Although June-bearing varieties generally give the better crop, they produce no crop at all the first year. For this reason, city growers will probably be more satisfied—at least, less impatient—with one of the everbearing varieties. Whichever variety you choose, plant it in the spring as early as the seed house delivers or as soon as the plants reach garden supply stores. If buying through a catalog, look for varieties particularly recommended for your region.

Several types of containers are available for growing a number of strawberry plants in a small space. Probably the most ambitious is a pyramid-type planter. It is really a set of three 5-inch-deep galvanized aluminum rings, the largest approximately 6 feet in diameter, and the second and third in descending size. (They are stacked atop one another.)

To prepare for planting, fill the first ring with soil, center the second ring on top of it, fill it with soil, then add the third ring and fill it. This triple-level planter will accommodate as many as 50 plants. It is equipped with sprinkler, tubing and hose connections; optional accessories include a plastic cover to protect plants from frost, and a net screen to protect the berries from an overenthusiastic flock of feathered fans.

If you can't spare a 6-foot space for the berries, try

a "strawberry jar." These are clay, pottery or ceramic vases with openings (pockets) in the sides where strawberry plants (herbs, succulents and other plants) may be tucked in. The jars can be found at garden stores and in some flower shops and department stores. They usually cost about $5 to $10.

Strawberry barrels are another possibility and are most attractive on a patio or balcony. Ordinary wooden kegs can sometimes be found at lumberyards or hardware stores. Have the sides of the barrel drilled with 1-inch diameter holes approximately 8 inches apart (best in staggered rows) to accommodate the plants. (If you don't have access to a drill, ask to have this done at the lumber store. They'll most likely be willing to do the job and for only a small charge.) Place the barrel in what will be its permanent spot; after it is filled with dirt and planted, it will be too heavy for you to move.

Place about a 2-inch layer of coarse gravel in the bottom of the barrel for drainage. Now take a mailing tube or a hollow pipe, or a piece of fairly stiff plastic rolled and fastened into a 2-inch wide cylinder, and stand it in the middle of the barrel. Fill the tube with gravel and keep it in place while you begin filling the barrel with the richest soil you have. Tuck the strawberry plants (from the outside in, roots first) into each hole as the soil level reaches it. Water as you go along. This will settle the soil and prevent the whole thing from slumping in later on. Continue until the barrel is filled and then space a few more plants on top. Now you can remove the cylinder from the center. The gravel core that remains will help water drain down through the barrel and out to the plants.

On a still smaller scale, a dozen plants in a 2-foot-square planter will produce some memorable "berries for breakfast" for a family of two or three.

It is important to plant strawberries at the proper depth—not too deep, not too shallow. Proper planting depth is at the level of the "crown"—an easily seen point which divides the tops from the roots.

After the plants are well established and begin to put out new growth, add a little soluble fertilizer to the water you give them. To help develop strong plants, pick off all flowers that appear until about the first of July (if you have the everbearing variety). Your plants should begin to bear about a month later. June-bearing varieties will begin to bloom in late April and May, but remember there will be no crop the first season they are planted.

Strawberries need too much sun to be grown successfully indoors, but they can be wintered over outdoors. As the weather grows cold, the plants will begin to grow dormant. They can withstand frost and light freezing, but should be protected against a hard freeze and severe weather. Covering the entire container with a tarpaulin will afford protection against cold; remove it when the weather warms.

Ozark Beauty. Everbearing; lush foliage; large, bright scarlet berries of good, sweet flavor.

ào **Ogallala.** Everbearing variety descended from the wild strawberry; combines hardiness with large berries of good flavor.

ào **Surecrop.** June-bearing variety; dependable and easy to grow; firm, deep red berry.

ào **Sparkle.** June-bearing; big, sweet and juicy. Can be planted close together in a patch and makes a good choice for a barrel.

ào **Sunrise.** June-bearing with large, bright berries; wonderful aroma and flavor.

Melons

Early-maturing and midget varieties can make melons a crop for container gardeners who have the space and are happy with a challenge that will deliver more fun than food.

The best melons come from long growing seasons and hot weather. You will need a big, deep container. Start seeds in 3-inch peat pots, indoors, in late April; put out after frost is past, but continue to bring in at night till evenings warm up, then transplant.

Even midget varieties need a lot of room—they will take as much as 4 feet in all directions if given the chance. To save space pinch out most of the lead runners—male flowers grow on them—this will give more lateral runners, with female flowers where fruit will form. You can train the vines up a trellis— if you also provide support for the growing melons. (A net bag, such as the kind that citrus is often packaged in, works fine as a sling for the fruit.)

Watermelon

New Hampshire Midget. Produces 5-pound fruit about 7 inches in diameter, good flavor but lots of seeds; ripens to a dark, dark green in about 75 days.

Sugar Baby. Round, 10-inch, 10-pound dark red flesh; not many seeds; very sweet-tasting; most popular of the small watermelons; takes 75 to 85 days.

Garden Baby. Similar to Sugar Baby, but fruit is a little larger, fewer seeds, and the vines are a little more compact. About 75 days.

Bushbaby. Pink-fleshed, 8-pound fruit has light green striped skin; borne on dwarf plants in 80 days.

Golden Midget. Light green skin turns yellow outside when the deep red flesh inside is ripe; takes 75 to 85 days.

Cantaloupe

Minnesota Midget. Miniature 4-inch fruits on small 3- to 4-foot vines in 60 days. Sweet, meaty, orange flesh; perfect for an individual serving.

꿈 **Cantaloupe Musketeer.** Compact plants measure only 2 to 3 feet across with 5½- to 6-inch round fruit in 3 months. Adapted to containers.

Honeydew

꿈 **Oliver's Pearl Cluster.** A first in honeydews: a bush form only 2 feet across. Needs long growing season—110 days. Sweet-tasting, delicious fruit.

Asparagus

Although asparagus provides more fun than food when planted in a container, don't let that keep you from trying. Asparagus is an interesting, easy plant to raise in a container and a real conversation piece. Plant several roots and plan on a party to celebrate the harvest of your crop a couple of years hence. You'll have to admit that such an event would classify as special!

Up until the last few years, asparagus roots were sold mainly through seed houses and nurseries, and usually in quantities of 25 roots or more. Today, you can often find them at local garden stands, packaged in quantities of as few as six. If you don't want or have room for six containers of asparagus, then share with a friend.

The root itself is interesting—thick, white tendrils stretch out from a center crown like the tentacles of an octopus The roots need to be spread out when planted, so you need a large container One 14 inches across the top and 11 inches deep will house one root. (Plastic trash baskets make inexpensive containers.)

Asparagus likes a rich diet, so to your ordinary potting mix you should add, per pot, an extra couple of tablespoons of a 5-10-5 fertilizer and a helping of cow manure. (Packaged dry cow manure can be found in garden centers or can be ordered through garden supply catalogs. It is to be mixed with water to form what is known in garden circles as manure "tea" and should be applied according to label directions. Packaged manure, enough to mix with water to make three gallons, costs about 65 cents; enough for 20 gallons is about $3.) In addition, the plants should be fed about every other week with your regular plant food.

The first spring after planting, only one or two asparagus spears will come up. Don't cut these. They will grow up tall, as high as 4 to 6 feet, filming out into feathery fern. In late summer, berries form on the ferns, and their bright orange-red color adds to the beauty of the plant.

As winter approaches, the plant dies down. Give final watering with manure tea and then hold off on any more water. Asparagus must have a dormant period that comes from a pronounced cold spell. Gardeners in the southern parts of the country where winters are warm and moist will not have luck with this vegetable.

As for severe winters, you can protect the roots from freezing by placing the pot in a sheltered spot, and/or by wrapping the pot with newspaper covered with plastic. Asparagus is a sturdy crop, and you will be able to take it through the winter with this simple protection.

The second year, and each succeeding year in the spring, feed again with 5-10-5 and liquid manure. You can begin harvesting the stalks as they appear. Don't let them grow more than 8 inches in height. If you have one container, you'll get only a few spears at a time, enough for a small side dish. Or you can blanch them in hot water for three to five minutes and freeze till you have enough for a meal. With several containers, you can have enough cuttings for that special asparagus party. The same roots will go on producing for 20 years or more, so once you start asparagus you can plan on a long-time, meaningful relationship with this plant!

❧ **Mary Washington.** Delicious, tender spears.

Rhubarb

Rhubarb makes a beautiful container plant. Handle much like asparagus, although the roots should be set a bit deeper, 3 to 4 inches under the top of the soil. Let the plant grow for a couple of years before taking cuttings of the stalks. Cut the fattest ones and leave

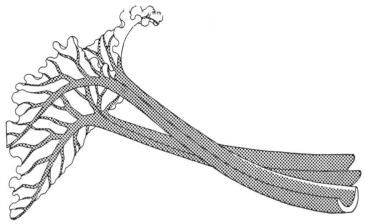

the skinny ones for the plant. Rhubarb stalks when grown in a pot can reach an inch in diameter; the same type of plant grown in the garden in full sun might produce stalks up to 2 inches in diameter. But a stalk or two of rhubarb, when combined with fresh strawberries, is a treat to make it worth growing. And in the meantime, rhubarb will make a large, dramatic ornamental plant. Huge green leaves and scarlet stalks make it an eye-opener. In the fall, the plant will die down and go dormant for the winter. Protect the roots from freezing temperatures as with asparagus.

Cabbage

Cabbage is an unlikely and therefore highly entertaining crop to grow in a container! One cabbage to an 8- to 10-inch container will allow the head to grow to full size. A wide bushel basket can accommodate a

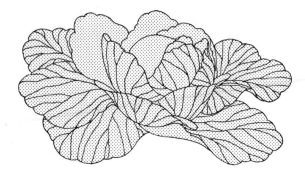

whole ring of one of the smaller varieties. (Plant carrots in the middle.)

Start cabbage seed five to seven weeks before the last frost date in spring; sow several seeds to each pot or spot. After the seeds sprout and grow to an inch or so, select the strongest seedling and prune out the others.

The main nemesis of cabbage is the same as for spinach or lettuce: heat. It is therefore best to choose early varieties that will develop before full summer comes on. The early varieties also require less space. Cabbages must have excellent drainage, lots of water, and regular feeding.

Consider planting a red cabbage (which is actually more purple than red). It tastes great and looks wonderful served by itself in a glass salad bowl.

In harvesting, leave the outer leaves and cut the heads so that a few inches of stalk are left; you will likely encourage new growth of a small loose head or two—a welcome addition to a salad or sandwich.

Days to maturity are counted from the transplant

stage. Allow about six weeks from seed to transplant stage.

ટ&& **Dwarf Morden.** A firm, round ball, 4 inches across and weighing only a pound. Lovely smooth leaves with light veining. Matures in about 55 days.

ટ&& **Baby Head.** Small, solid heads only 2½ to 3 pounds; crisp and white inside; takes 72 days.

ટ&& **Cabbage Darkri.** Nice 6- to 8-inch heads of creamy light green; only a few outer leaves so you can tuck more plants into a container; about 47 days.

ટ&& **Ruby Ball.** All-America selection; a beautiful, perfectly round, ball-shaped head; few wrapper leaves; matures early and fast (65 days); in container grows to about 3 pounds but capable of up to 5 pounds.

ટ&& **Red Acre.** A small, under 3-pound head; round, hard and deep purple throughout; takes 80 days to maturity. Plants are small, short-stemmed, compact, and look pretty in a container.

ટ&& **Mammoth Red Rock.** If you have a long enough cool season and are going to devote a container or more to cabbage anyway, you might as well go for a big one. This is it. Takes 95 days; can measure up to 7 inches across and weigh up to 7 pounds; comes across strong with its big flattened globe head. Use a larger container—about a 2-gallon size.

See Oriental Vegetables for Chinese cabbage.

Jerusalem Artichokes

Practically no one thinks of the Jerusalem artichoke as a container plant, and yet the yield per pot (better, a tub) is as high as for any crop with the possible exception of the tomato. It is easy to grow and one plant produces a number of potato-like tubers that can be baked, boiled, creamed, pickled or eaten raw.

The Jerusalem artichoke, a relative of the sunflower, grows as high as 6 feet, with bright yellow blossoms 2 to 3 inches across in late summer. When the plant begins to die down, the tubers can be dug up. (Leave at least one in the pot, mulch for the winter, and expect a new plant in the spring.)

Though the tubers look a good deal like potatoes, they have a somewhat nutty flavor and can substitute for water chestnuts in Chinese dishes. When steamed and creamed, they have a delicate flavor not unlike cauliflower. They do not store as well as potatoes, so they should be dug up only as they are to be used.

Oriental Vegetables

A number of different kinds of similar plants go by the name (sometimes mistakenly) of Chinese cabbage,

Chinese celery or Chinese mustard. By whatever name, they are wonderful vegetables that can be grown singly in 6- to 10-inch pots, in a thick circle in a big round tub or spread out in a row in a planter box. They look terrific, and they take up less space than our Western cabbage.

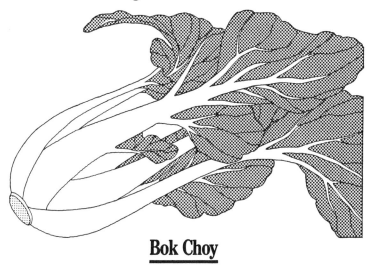

Bok Choy

Bok choy, also known as Chinese mustard, and in Cantonese as pak choi, is a beautiful vegetable for close-up gardening. Its thick white stalks are somewhat like celery, but they are not ribbed or fibrous. The creamy white and tender central stems are topped with large, dark green, spoon-shaped leaves.

Bok choy is tender and mild-tasting and most often used cooked rather than raw, in soups and stir-fry. No bowl of won ton soup is quite so good without bok choy.

This vegetable needs to grow fast, or hot weather will turn the taste bitter, and the plants will bolt (go to seed). Plant early in the spring, water generously every day and use a high nitrogen fertilizer every two weeks. Harvest before the days get too long. Be sure to plant more seeds than needed for the container—after the seedlings are up and growing, thin them out over a period of time. The thinnings can be eaten in salads or in stir-fry dishes and soups. For fall harvest, start in a shaded area in August, move to sunny spot in September. In the Deep South and Pacific Coast, seeds can be planted in fall and winter for favorable results.

Bok choy can be eaten anytime after it sprouts, but let it get big enough to make your efforts worthwhile. When stalks are about 8 inches tall, slip a collar (a half-gallon milk carton with both ends cut off will do) over plant to blanch (keep them light colored).

Lei Choi. Plant grows 15 to 18 inches tall in about 47 days from sowing; pure white, spicy-tasting stalks, 10 to 14 to a plant.

Crispy Choy. Earlier than Lei Choi by almost a week; a smaller plant, with a more pungent flavor; its 8 to 12 greenish-white stalks grow 7 to 8 inches tall.

Wong Bok

Wong bok, also known as siew choy in Cantonese, most often goes by the name of Chinese cabbage. It

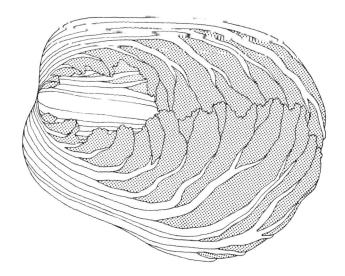

actually looks like a cross between cabbage and celery, but its flavor is very different from either—mild and distinctive. Its leaves are tightly curled into a stalklike head, and its inner leaves are creamy white.

Wong bok is a wonderful vegetable that can make it to full-grown size in a little more than two months (70 days from seed). It is a good choice if you don't have a whole lot of direct sun, since it does well in partial shade.

Michihli

Michihli, also called chihli or green Chinese cabbage, has a looser, greener head than wong bok; something like a cross between celery and cos or romaine lettuce. In Cantonese it is called ching siew choy, and the name Michihli also refers to a specific variety. These cabbages are taller and slimmer than wong bok, have a stronger, more pungent taste, and can be cured with vinegar and salt for a spicy relish. A head weighs 3 to 4 pounds. Try one to a 6- to 8-inch pot, or provide a comparable amount of room for several in a bigger container.

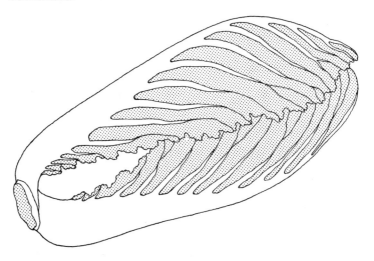

Michihli. Heads grow to 18 inches tall, 3½ inches across; usually grown for the fall. Plant mid-July or after, so that the shorter days will encourage formation of solid heads instead of tall flower stalks and seeds; takes 70 days.

Jade Pagoda. A newer variety than Michihli; medium green, crinkled outer leaves and heart of creamy yellow. Grows 16 inches tall and 6 inches thick after about 70 days.

꒰꒱ **Two Seasons Hybrid.** Good heat resistance and fast maturing (62 days), so spring planting is possible; but it's still trickier to get a crop when heading into long days of summer heat.

Sprouts

Here is the fastest seed-to-table crop you can grow—as speedy as 3 or 4 days. A number of different seeds can be used for sprouts. The ones listed below are some of the most popular.

꒰꒱ **For sprouts from beans.** Wash the beans well and sort through them as you would if cooking. Soak overnight in cold water; drain. Put the beans in a jar with a screw-top lid (with holes punched in it so the water can be drained off). You can buy special sprout jars or jar lids, or recycle a dark amber or brown glass jar such as those used for some brands of applesauce or baked beans. The idea is to shade the beans from light, which will turn the sprouts a light pink or green—creamy white sprouts are what you are after. Rinse and drain the beans well each morning and evening. Place the jar in a dark place to prevent exposure to daylight. The sprouts should be ready to eat in 4 or 5 days and should be harvested no later than 7 days. They will keep for a few more days in the refrigerator if stored in a closed plastic bag. A pound of beans will produce about 4 pounds of sprouts; try sprouting about ½ cup at a time.

ટ▲ **For sprouting smaller seeds.** No need to soak overnight. Put seeds in jar; cover with water and let stand for a few minutes, then drain. Rinse and drain each day as above. Put a piece of cheesecloth over the top as you drain the seeds if the holes in the lid are too large. No need to store these sprouts away from light; you'll want the small green leaves to develop before eating.

ટ▲ **Mung bean.** The chop suey bean sprout. Provides a crunchy, nutritious treat in sandwiches and salads as well as in Oriental dishes; good to eat raw or cooked. Look for untreated seeds. Mung beans take about 3 to 5 days to sprout.

ટ▲ **Soy bean.** Not much difference between green or yellow seed; highly favored by the nutrition-minded; takes just 3 to 5 days.

ટ▲ **Garden cress, curled cress or pepper grass.** These are the sprouts that, along with thin slices of cucumber, can make plain old bread-and-butter sand-wiches elegant. Grows rapidly; enjoy in 3 to 5 days. Seeds can also be sprouted on sponge or moist cotton. Grow in bonsai trays or flats on a window sill in temperatures under 68°. Harvest seedlings when 6 inches high.

ટ▲ **Mustard.** Same as cress, and delicious.

ટ▲ **Fenugreek.** A relative of the bean and pea family

that looks a lot like clover; popular for sprouting because of its nutrition and taste—a spicy sort of curry flavor when eaten shortly after sprouting; 3 to 5 days.

Oriental Cucumbers

These cucumbers grow long and slim and the flesh is firm, crisp and white. Most of the plants have a strong tendency to climb and will grow best if they have something to cling to. Grow them on a railing or trellis so the cucumbers can hang down, and they will grow long and straight where intended. (Some varieties are curved.) Plant in spring, 1 inch deep. They like lots of sun, especially morning sun. Give lots of water. Don't pick too soon; wait till the fruit reaches its minimum length.

🙰 **Kyoto.** Long and thin; 2 feet in length; in 62 days.

🙰 **Sooyow.** Early, dark green, delicious, with fruit 10 to 12 inches long; highly spined and ribbed; 60 days.

🙰 **Yamoto Extra Long.** Produces straight, smooth-skinned, dark green cucumbers, 18 to 24 inches long in 65 days.

Oriental Radishes

These radishes, known in Japanese as daikon, and in Chinese as lo bok, are used in the Orient in many different ways—pickled, battered and fried in hot oil, finely shredded and used as a nest for raw fish. We're talking here about BIG radishes; some can weigh as much as 30 pounds (Sakurajima, a big globe-shaped radish), and others can reach nearly 3 feet in length (Nerima's long white root grows 2½ feet long). If 30-pound or 3-foot radishes are not what you had in mind, there are smaller oriental radishes you can choose.

Pax. A cross between Japanese and European types. Root 6 to 8 inches long, straight and tapering; 28 days to tender, crunchy, spicy eating.

Summer Cross Hybrid. A white radish that takes 45 days; root is ready to eat at 6 inches but can grow to 14 inches if given the container depth. Plant in spring or fall.

White Chinese (Celestial). Crisp and mild-flavored winter radish which must have cool weather at end of growing season, so should be planted in midsummer for fall and early winter harvest. Pure white root is 6 to 8 inches long, 3 inches across. Takes 60 days.

Oriental Eggplant

This eggplant, also known as nasu, is long and slender with a much more delicate, delicious, distinctive (mushroom-like) taste than its globular American counterpart. The tubular shape makes for slices of more uniform size, also. These plants like hot weather and need to be kept warm from the start. Keep on a sunny window sill until warm enough to go outdoors, but then move them indoors at night if you must protect them from cool nights. They are hard to get started and won't take off at all if it is too cool for them. Pick off the first few early flowers so that energy goes to fruit production. Fruits have a very thin skin and are soft and delicate.

🐚 **Ichiban Hybrid.** Slender, Oriental-type eggplant up to 12 inches long; great tasting. Matures in 61 to 65 days, several weeks earlier than American types, and sets lots more fruit per plant (growers report as many as 60 or 70 to a plant).

Shungiku

This plant is a member of the chrysanthemum family, frequently called the garland chrysanthemum, and also known as the chop suey green. Like other chrysanthemums, it likes cool weather. Culture is easy, like that for spinach. Will produce leaves long enough to harvest (5 inches long) in six to seven weeks. Plant will resprout. Leaves are stringy and taste too strong if plant is left to mature. It does grow quickly as an ornamental, though, and will produce dozens of small yellow flowers. Sow seed every few weeks for eating, and then let plant go to bloom. Use leaves raw in small amounts in salads, soups and stir-fry dishes; has a milder flavor when cooked.

Chinese Parsley

This is coriander, also called Mexican parsley or cilantro. If you grow parsley, plant coriander, too. It is easy to grow and difficult to find fresh on the market, an added incentive. The flat, fan-shaped leaves are similar to Italian parsley and are used as a garnish in Oriental dishes and for seasoning barbecued chicken and duck.

Coriander likes cool temperatures; can be planted early in spring or late in summer for the leaves. If you want to raise the plant for its tiny seeds, which when crushed are somewhat orangy in flavor, plant in early spring and gather seeds in late summer. Grows 1½ to 2 feet tall.

Snow Peas

Our new dwarf "sugar snap" peas, or edible-podded peas, are not really of Chinese origin, but no matter—they are delicious, expensive to buy fresh in the market, and make a good choice for home-grown. Peas cannot take heat, and should be started as early as possible so they can be grown and harvested before hot weather comes along.

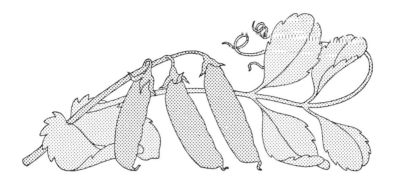

For quick start, soak peas overnight. Also soak the soil before planting the peas. Plant lots of seed—for a planter box 7 inches wide and 3 feet long, you might plant 100 to 150 seeds (about 3 to 4 times what is usually recommended). However, the cost of the seed is not much and some of them will die and some will not grow well. That's just the way it is with peas.

Watering is critical while the pods are forming, so keep the plants moist to keep them growing fast. Tie vines to support with soft twine when about 12 inches high. Peas are lovely at blossoming stage, and ugly afterwards. As soon as the pods mature, there is no saving the vines, so don't regard them as anything but the most transient screen or décor.

The harvest time for the newer dwarf edible-pod varieties is not as critical as it is for the older types. Still, keep your eye on the pods. For the older varieties, the moment the pods begin to swell is the time when they are tenderest, sweet and crunchy. Almost overnight, they can begin to toughen. The time is not so limited for harvesting the newer varieties and the peas can be allowed to fill out the pod for a longer period.

ॐ **Sugar Snap.** Edible pod, climbs on trellis; a balcony railing will do if you weave twine between posts for horizontal support. This variety was the breakthrough in edible pods at greater maturity. Produces short pods, only 2½ to 3 inches long. Vines can grow as high as 4 feet and will need support. Reaches full maturity at 70 days.

ॐ **Sugar Ann.** An All-America selection developed from the earlier Sugar Snap pea. Designed for small space. Bushy-type growth with plant reaching a height of only 18 to 30 inches. Its dwarf, compact vines can be trained easily to a low 2-foot-high fence if necessary; 56 days.

ॐ **Mammoth Melting Sugar.** The long-time standard for edible-podded peas. Light green vines growing 4 to 4½ feet tall produce large, tender pods 4 to 5 inches long. Produces more per unit of space than others. Plant early, needs to be staked and sheltered from the wind. Pick often for best production and pick when pods are just beginning to fill out; 74 days.

ॐ **Dwarf White Sugar.** A bush type, easier for most container gardening with vines only 2 to 2½ feet tall. Several plants to a pot will support one another and not need staking; 65 days.

Snowbird. Dwarf plants 16 to 18 inches tall do not need support. Good where cool season is short and limited space available. Heavy producer; 3-inch-long pods; 58 days.

Sugar Bon. New and only 18 inches tall; no staking needed; especially suited for limited space. Can make a pretty, early spring border around a balcony or patio; 56 days.

GROWTH CHART

For specific information developed by your state climatologist on average last and first frost dates for your area, check with your local Weather Service Office (some 300 offices around the country), listed in the phone book under U. S. Government, Department of Commerce.

GROWTH CHART

CROP	CONTAINER REQUIREMENTS	GROWING SEASON
BEETS	Any allowing soil depth of 10 to 12 inches	cool weather—early spring, fall
BUSH BEANS	Any having 8 to 10 inches of soil	warm weather
CABBAGE	8 to 10 inches wide; 6 inches deep	cool weather—early spring
CARROTS	Any with depth of variety selected plus 2 inches (10 to 12 inches of soil usually ample)	cool weather—early spring, fall
CUCUMBERS	Gallon size for one hill; 5- gallon size for 3 or 4 hills; hanging basket good for single plant	warm weather
EGGPLANT	Not less than 3-gallon size; use 12- to 14-inch diameter pot for each plant	warm weather
KOHLRABI	6 to 8 inches wide	cool weather
LETTUCE	Any type container suitable; size determined by quantity	cool weather; can stand light frost
MELONS	Minimum: bushel basket	warm weather
ONIONS	Any type container suitable; should be 8 to 10 inches deep for green onions	cool weather; can stand light frost
PEPPERS	Not less than gallon size per bell-type plant; 8- to 10-inch diameter for hot	warm weather
RADISHES	Any type container suitable; should be at least 6 inches deep	cool weather; can stand light frost
SNOW PEAS	8 to 10 inches wide for 20 to 25 seeds	cool weather
SPINACH	An 8- to 10-inch pot per plant	cool weather—early spring, fall
SQUASH	At least 5-gallon size for each 3- or 4-plant hill (bushel basket, garbage can & washtub are practical)	warm weather; will produce through fall
TOMATOES	Dwarf types in gallon size; standard varieties need 2- to 3-gallon size; miniatures can make it in an 8- to 10-inch pot.	warm weather

WHERE TO MAKE INITIAL PLANTING	WHEN TO MAKE INITIAL PLANTING	DAYS FROM SEED TO HARVEST	APPROXIMATE AVERAGE SIZE OF MATURE PLANT
directly into container	2 to 4 weeks before frost-free date	50 to 60	10 to 12 inches tall
directly into container	early spring	snap 50 to 55; broad 85	1 to 2 feet fall
in peat pots for early start	6 weeks before last frost date	65 to 95	4 to 6 inches for midget sizes
directly into container	2 to 4 weeks before frost-free date	65 to 75	10 to 12 inches tall
in peat pots for early start	3 to 4 weeks before frost-free date	55 to 70	vines can be shaped by pinching back
in peat pots for early start	8 to 9 weeks before transplant time	120 to 140	1 to 3 feet tall
directly into container	2 to 4 weeks before frost-free date	45 to 60	12 to 18 inches tall
directly into container	4 to 6 weeks before frost-free date	40 to 50	6 to 10 inches tall
3-inch peat pots for early start	late April	75 to 90	2 to 5 feet across
directly into container	4 to 6 weeks before frost-free date	35 to 45 days from sets to green onion	10 to 12 inches tall
in peat pots for early start	7 to 8 weeks before frost-free date	110 to 120	2 to 3 feet tall
directly into container	2 to 4 weeks before frost-free date	24 to 30	6 to 8 inches tall
directly into container	3 to 4 weeks before frost-free date	58 to 68	2 to 4 feet tall
directly into container	2 to 4 weeks before frost-free date	50 to 70	plants spread out, grow only a few inches tall
in peat pots for early start	3 to 4 weeks before frost-free date	summer: 50 to 60 winter: 85 to 110	bush type: 2 to 3 feet tall vine type: controlled by pinching
in peat pots	6 to 8 weeks before frost-free date	90 to 130, depending on type	dwarf type: 2 to 3 feet tall standard varieties: 3 to 5 feet tall

CATALOGS

One of the most delightful parts of gardening is the time spent in catalog browsing. The catalogs listed below are sources for the varieties mentioned in this book. While all of them offer seeds that with proper care can be grown in all parts of the country, some varieties are adapted especially for certain climes. Gardeners in the northern states, therefore, might want to include in their reading a seed catalog from that part of the country; southern gardeners might do the same for their region.

✓ **Burpee Gardens**
Warminster, PA
18974

Probably the granddaddy of them all, this handbook-size catalog lists hundreds and hundreds of varieties. It is well-organized, allows one-stop shopping for what you'll need—and is not nearly as much fun to read as many of the others.

✓ **D. V. Burrell Seed**
Growers Co.
Rocky Ford, CO
81067

The farmer is the major outlet for this seed grower, but the company also offers small quantities of a large number of varieties that are suitable for the home gardener.

✓ **Comstock,**
Ferre & Co.
263 Main St.
Wethersfield, CT
06109

The folks at this company, which traces its beginnings to 1820, describe their catalog as credible not fancy. It is also easy to read and carries a good selection of the best of the old and new, a good herb list, and a selection of small vegetables for container gardens.

√ **William Dam Seeds**
P.O. Box 8400
Dundas, Ontario,
    Canada L9H 6M1

This company continues to remain a small family business after 35 years, concentrating on seeds for the home gardener and hobbyist. Its Dutch-immigrant origins are reflected in the number of European selections offered along with a number of this country's favorites. A good selection of herbs and garden aids as well.

√ **Farmer Seed and**
    Nursery Co.
Fairbault, MN 55021

Another long-established firm with up-to-date selections. Features a collection of midget vegetables; offers the dwarf blueberry, Tophat, and dwarf apple trees for northern climes.

Gardener's Eden
P.O. Box 7307
San Francisco, CA
    94120

No seeds or plants here, just wonderful accessories for gardening—many ideal for the small-space gardener. You'll find tubs and trellises, beautiful pots and planters, practical gloves and gadgets.

√ **Grace's Gardens**
10 Bay Street
Westport, CT 06880

This small leaflet lists Chinese, Italian and Mexican seeds, some interesting tomatoes and a few fun-to-grow plants—from a yard-long bean to a fragrant mignonette.

√ **Gurney Seed &**
    Nursery Co.
Yankton, SD 57079

This catalog is almost tabloid-size and presents a colorful jumble of offerings that will have you turning back and forth, poking around through hundreds of items, much the way you might in an old-time country store. The company is nearly 120 years old, but its offerings are up-to-date and the catalog is fun to read if you're not uptight and in a hurry—which catalog browsing can help fix.

√ **Harris Seeds**
Moreton Farm—
3670 Buffalo Rd.
Rochester, NY 14624

A long-time seed company with its own research staff and a large following among commercial growers, also publishes an excellent home gardening catalog. You'll find many of the most popular varieties here, and the company prides itself on its competitive prices.

Hastings
P.O. Box 4274
Atlanta, GA 30302

One of the most informative, attractive and useful catalogs a gardener could hope for. This company, approaching its 100th birthday, concentrates on varieties that do well in southern climes, and flags varieties that have been especially selected as "space savers." A discriminating selection of wonderful, proven-variety vegetables, herbs, berries, miniature fruits—even a kiwi vine.

√ **Le Jardin du Gourmet**
P.O. Box 104
West Danville, VT
05873

Here is a small seed company that the small-space gardener can identify with. The catalog, a leaflet really, offers 20-cent, sample packets of a fairly large number of vegetables and herbs—a great idea for gardeners who want to experiment or who need only a few seeds. Also offered are tempting vegetable varieties from France, Holland, Germany and a number of other countries, along with a potpourri of other goodies, such as teas and truffles in tins.

√ **J. W. Jung Seed Co.**
Randolph, WI 53957

A big, magazine-size catalog from a 75-year-old company that offers many of the newcomers while retaining many of the old-timers. Vegetables, herbs, berries, all kinds of garden aids.

√ **Kitazawa Seed Co.**
236 W. Taylor St.
San Jose, CA 95110

A small 3-page leaflet lists hard-to-find, Oriental vegetables—beans, cabbages, cucumbers, eggplant, squash, radishes and a few melons.

The Krider Nurseries
P.O. Box 29
Middlebury, IN
46540

The catalog from this old, established Middle Western garden center features ornamental plants, but also includes a selection of berries and dwarf fruit trees.

√ **Earl May Seed &**
Nursery Co.
Shenandoah, IA
51603

Here is another great catalog—earnest, straightforward, packed with selections in a wide range of vegetables, fruits, berries, garden aids, herbs, specialties—all well-described and illustrated in color.

Mellinger's
2310 W. South Range
North Lima, OH
44452

This great big no-nonsense catalog is crammed with offerings and is especially good for locating all kinds of garden aids, including containers (the Vegi-Tub, for example). Not much description of the plants, so best to know the varieties you want. Vegetables, herbs, Oriental and specialty crops, dwarf fruit trees.

Miller Nurseries
Canandaigua, NY
14424

A wonderful, full-color catalog showing off dwarf fruit trees of all kinds, including citrus, and lots of berries. Garden aids, too. Need a container for your tree? This catalog offers used wine barrels cut in half.

✓ **Nichols Herb and**
Rare Seeds
1190 North Pacific
Hwy.
Albany, OR 97321

Not a single color photo here; you get simple black-and-white line drawings on recycled paper pages that have been stapled together. So what makes this an attractive, absolutely great catalog? Clear helpful text and a large selection of herbs; a wide and varied selection of vegetables including new and unusual varieties as well as Oriental and other specialties.

✓ **L. L. Olds Seed Co.**
P.O. Box 7790
Madison, WI 53707

A great big catalog from a century-old company that offers the works—vegetables, berries, fruit trees, herbs, garden aids. Varieties suitable for container growing are specifically indicated in the various sections.

✓ **Geo. W. Park Seed**
Co., Inc.
P.O. Box 31
Greenwood, SC
29646

A great catalog by a great company that pioneered the development of compact vegetables especially suited to limited-space or container gardening. Includes all the vegetables, some berries, and many specialty vegetables such as Oriental and Mexican. A high percentage of offerings are illustrated in color photographs.

✓ **Pinetree Garden Seeds**
RR 1, Box 397
New Gloucester, ME
04260

A charming, small catalog highlighting "space efficient" plants. Offers untreated seeds in small-size packets, so you can afford to experiment with a number of different varieties. The number of seeds to the packet is noted for each vegetable type. This is not a lavish catalog; it is small, earnest, informative—and the people who put it together know what they're talking about.

✓ **Rayner Brothers Inc.**
Salisbury, MD 21801

Strawberries are the stars of this catalog but there are a number of other good choices, too. Dwarf fruit trees, other berries, grapes, rhubarb and asparagus, even horseradish. Several pages of instruction on how to grow strawberries and blueberries, as well as hints on growing other crops such as asparagus and bramble berries.

✓ **R. H. Shumway's**
Rockford, IL 61105

Colorful, old-fashioned, magazine-size catalog from one of the oldest seed companies in the country—boasting seven generations of customers. Offers a wide selection of vegetables and offers special collections called "super savers," featuring seeds for the salad bowl garden or the dinner plate special or gourmet garden.

Stark Bro's Nurseries
& Orchards
Louisiana, MO 63353

The large, colorful catalog from this major fruit-tree nursery features miniature and dwarf-size fruit trees among hundreds of varieties offered. Also good selection of berries.

✓ **Thompson & Morgan Inc.**
P.O. Box 100
Farmingdale, NJ
07727

Your commitment to edible crops might waver as you leaf your way through the flower section of this beautiful catalog, but do press on because the vegetable and herb goodies in the back are just as lovely. Hard-to-find European varieties and other good choices for the container gardener are here.

✓ **Tsang & Ma**
1306 Old Country
Road
Belmont, CA 94002

You will find a good choice of the most popular Oriental vegetables in this four-page brochure, and good value, too. Other choices to tempt you include "everything you need for a Chinese kitchen"—from clay pots and bamboo steamers to chop sticks and stoneware.

✓ **Vermont Bean**
Seed Co.
Garden Lane
Bomoseen, VT 05732

You will find a lot more than beans in the catalog from this company. The more than 70 varieties of beans—from Swedish brown beans to Red Mexican beans—are merely the prelude to a comprehensive selection of other vegetables, including many of the hard-to-find, old-fashioned varieties. These people are serious gardeners.

HOME GROWING RECORD

DATE PLANTED	TYPE & VARIETY PLANTED

Home Growing Record

PROGRESS	DATE HARVESTED	RESULTS

141

DATE PLANTED	TYPE & VARIETY PLANTED

PROGRESS	DATE HARVESTED	RESULTS